RIDING THE RETIRE ROLLER COASTER

By
RUTH KLEMM

Table of Contents

Chapter 1: New Beginnings 1
    Flashback: One Week Ago 4
    Present Day: Decision Made 6
    The Chaos of Cleaning Out 8
    Saying Goodbye... 10

Chapter 2: Packing Up and Moving On 15
    The Packing Chaos Begins 18
    The Dog-Related Travel Adventures......... 20
    First Impressions of Delaware 23

Chapter 3: Settling In: Unpacking A Journey Through Chaos.. 27
    Day One of Settling In: The Coffee Quest 27
    The Shower Curtain Saga 29
    Making New Friends… Sort Of 30
    Unpacking Roulette 32
    Home Is Where the Weird Is 32
    The Unexpected Guests 33

Chapter 4: The Quest for Friendship............... 36

Copyright© 2024 by Ruth Klemm

ALL RIGHTS RESERVED. No part of this book may be reproduced or transmitted in any form by any means, electronic or mechanical, including photocopying and recording, or by any information storage and retrieval system, except as may be expressly permitted in writing from the author.

The Potluck Perils 40

Awkward Encounters 41

Friendships in New York vs. Delaware: A Study in Contrasts 42

Making the Rounds 43

The Great "Welcome to the Neighborhood" Gift 44

Murphy's Role in the Quest 45

The Quest Continues 47

The First Playdate 48

Chapter 5: Embracing Change 49

The Heat Is On 49

The Emotional Rollercoaster 51

Wardrobe Malfunctions 53

The Great Underwear Dilemma 54

Light-Hearted Tips for Survival 55

Conclusion: Finding the Joy in Chaos 57

Chapter 6: Asthmatic Love and Unstoppable Passion 58

Pee-gasms: A Hidden Perk of Hysterectomy 60

Falling for Fran :Burnt Cheese and Burnt Inhalers............... 64

Recovery Wins and Ridiculous Excuses ... 65

Chapter 7: Rediscovering Love 67

Love Letters and Shared Interests.............. 68

Rediscovering Love: The Real-Life Rollercoaster 69

The Real Treasures of Midlife Romance... 70

Conclusion: Love, Laughter, and the Air Fryer Chronicles................................ 71

Chapter 8: Adventures in Marriage.................. 72

Breakfast Battles: The Culinary Showdown 72

Canine Chaos: The Great Dog Race 74

Chore Wars: The Battle of the Brooms 76

Date Night Adventures: The Quest for Culinary Delights.............................. 77

Laughing Through Life: Love in the Madness 79

Chapter 9: Embracing New Experiences.......... 81

The Great Retirement Adventure............... 81

The Clay Chronicles 82

Culinary Capers 83
Road Trip Ruckus 84
Conclusion: Embracing the Absurdity 86
Ice Skating Shenanigans 87
Culinary Explorations: The Restaurant Roulette 88
Dog Park Antics: The Canine Chronicles .. 90
Surprises on the Road: A Mini-Road Trip. 92
Embracing the Joy of New Adventures 93

Chapter 10: The Great Outdoors 95
Embracing Nature's Quirks 95
The Dog Walk Chronicles 96
The Beach Trip Disaster 98
Wildlife Encounters 100
Embracing the Charm of Delaware 102
Unforgettable Quirks 103
The Adventure Continues 104

Chapter 11: Life Lessons and Reflections 106
The Journey So Far 106
Comedic Reflections on Aging 107

Heartwarming Anecdotes of Friendship and Love 108
Aging: Funny and Liberating 110
The Blessing of a Happy Life 111
The Legacy of Laughter 112
The Golden Years: More Than Just a Phase 113
The Circle of Friendship 114
Cherishing Every Moment 115

Chapter 1: New Beginnings

A lifetime supplies of fruitcake. I mean, who even eats fruitcake? It's like the mystery meat of desserts!

So, there I was, staring at that retirement offer like it was a Tinder date gone wrong. "Swipe right for freedom, swipe left for more meetings about Peter's 'innovative' ideas." Just as I was about to hit send, my phone buzzed. It was my buddy Jim, who's been retired for a solid five minutes.

"Hey! What's it like?" I asked, half-excited, half-terrified.

"Like a permanent vacation," Jim replied. "Except nobody tells you that the beach is just your living room, and the only waves are the ones you make while trying to get out of the recliner."

"Sounds amazing," I said, suppressing the urge to laugh. "But what do you do all day?"

"Mostly just binge-watching shows and arguing with the cat over who gets the sunny spot on the couch. Sometimes I throw a little gardening in there, but my plants think I'm just a weird sunbather."

I chuckled.

Ahh, now...

Turning 66 ½ and hitting that 50-year mark of non-stop work. For most, it's a milestone that screams, "Time for orthopedic shoes and daily vitamin supplements!" But for me? It was like reaching the top of a mountain... only to realize the guide forgot the snacks. Fifty years of work! You'd think they'd throw a parade or at least offer a commemorative mug that says, "Congrats, You Survived!" Instead, it was just me, staring down the barrel of retirement like a curious raccoon eyeing a closed trash can have intrigued but unsure if it's really worth the effort to pry it open.

Retirement had always felt like some distant relative you politely nod at from across the room. But there it was, knocking on my door, holding a neon sign that read: "Freedom!" Or maybe it was just a neon sticky note because, let's face it, those HR budgets aren't exactly known for extravagance.

One morning, I received an email about early retirement. It arrived like an email from a Nigerian prince thrilling and slightly suspicious. "I mean, retirement already?" I thought. "That's for trust-fund kids who own private islands, not folks like me who've been waging war against overgrown hedges and fighting rising utility bills since 1983!"

The decision should've been simple, right? No more meetings about Peter's "revolutionary" ideas that are just recycled suggestions from 1994. But when I saw that email, I felt like I was caught between taking a golden ticket to freedom and getting stuck with a lifetime supply of tapioca pudding.

I took a deep breath, stared back at that email, and thought, "Well, at least I'd get to do it all without a dress code!" And if nothing else, I'd finally have time to find out if those orthopedic shoes really were as comfy as they claimed.

Flashback: One Week Ago

I was in the breakroom, staring at the world's slowest coffee machine as if it held the answers to life itself. Just as I took my first sip of the lukewarm brew, I heard a familiar, overly chirpy voice: "Hey there!" It was Karen from HR, her voice so peppy you'd think she was the love child of Snow White and a Care Bear. I braced myself. Karen never brought good news or donuts, for that matter.

"So," she dragged the word like a cat playing with a mouse, "I've been reviewing your file." Oh no. I was convinced this was it. I was finally getting canned for that time I called the annual review a "colossal waste of perfectly good oxygen." But instead, she smiled wider, as if she'd just won Employee of the Month… again. "Guess what? You're eligible for early retirement!" She clapped her hands as if I'd just won the HR Lottery. "Isn't that just thrilling?"

I blinked, trying to figure out if this was a dream or if someone had spiked my coffee. "Early retirement?" I repeated, the words feeling as foreign as a vegan hot dog. "Yes! We're restructuring, and you're one of the lucky few!" She beamed like she was on commission for every employee she convinced to exit early. "Lucky few," I muttered, wondering if this was HR code for "We need your parking spot." But Karen had already flitted off like an HR fairy, off to tell the next victim I mean, lucky winner.

Left alone with my now-bitter coffee, I felt a mix of panic and amusement. Retirement meant freedom, sure, but also the terrifying realization that I might soon become one of those retirees who name their houseplants after TV characters. "Meet my ficus, Gandalf, and this here is my fern, Hermione!" Did I even have a bucket list? And if I did, was it just a glorified to-do list with "Don't die" at the top?

I pictured myself at a retirement party, people gathered around, clapping politely while I awkwardly accepted a clock with a picture of the office on it. "Thanks, everyone! I'll treasure this as a reminder of how I wasted countless hours here instead of napping!"

Suddenly, I could hear Karen's voice in my head. "Just think of all the free time you'll have! You can take up knitting!" Knitting?! I didn't even know how to tie my shoelaces without a YouTube tutorial! The only thing I ever knitted was an argument with my lawnmower.

As I took another sip of my lukewarm coffee, I realized I needed a plan. Maybe I could start a blog: "The Adventures of a Recently Retired Guy Who Still Can't Figure Out How to Work the TV Remote." Or maybe I could start a support group for retirees struggling to remember what day it is. "Hi, I'm Dave, and I've been retired for two weeks... and I still think it's Monday."

With a sigh, I glanced at the coffee machine. "Guess I'll just have to brew up some courage," I muttered, wondering how many more cups it would take before I figured this whole retirement thing out.

PRESENT DAY: DECISION MADE

I was, staring at that same email like it was a bad breakup text. I could either slog through another decade of performance reviews, awkward holiday parties, and pretending to care about Peter's passion for "team synergy," or I could press "accept" and step into the unknown.

But what would I do? Learn to bake sourdough? Please! I'd probably end up with a loaf that could double as a doorstop. Take up birdwatching? I'd just spend all my time complaining about how many sparrows there were compared to exotic birds. "Excuse me, nature, where are all the flamingos? I didn't sign up for a sparrow convention!"

Maybe I'd become the "lady who lunches" you know, the polished type who discusses Pilates and organic kale at chic cafes. I could see it now: "Oh, darling, have you tried the gluten-free, non-GMO, ethically sourced quinoa salad? It's divine!" Spoiler alert: it wouldn't be me.

With a deep breath and a click of the mouse, I accepted. It felt like bungee-jumping off a corporate cliff, only I wasn't sure if I'd land in a hot tub or a pile of stress balls. Either way, it was done.

As I hit "send," I half-expected a confetti cannon to go off or at least a marching band to parade by my cubicle. But instead, it was just silence like the moment after you accidentally send a text meant for your best friend to your boss.

"Congratulations on your leap into retirement!" I imagined Karen from HR saying with her trademark enthusiasm. "Now you can really embrace the 'you' you've always wanted to be! Just remember: no more office gossip!"

Yeah, right! I'd have to find a new group of retirees to gossip with about how the only thing worse than overcooked broccoli is a too-bright retirement community. "Did you hear what Gladys said about the new shuffleboard rules? Scandalous!"

I leaned back in my chair, feeling a mix of excitement and dread. Retirement might be the ultimate adventure or it could just turn me into that eccentric neighbor who throws a weekly tea party for imaginary friends. Either way, I was ready to embrace it. After all, what's life without a little risk? And if it all went south, at least I could finally perfect my sourdough doorstop!

THE CHAOS OF CLEANING OUT

The next day, it was time to clear my desk an adventure worthy of its own reality TV show, "Survivor: Cubicle Edition." Each drawer was like an archaeological dig, revealing relics from decades of professional survival.

First drawer: notepads. So many notepads. Apparently, I'd believed I was going to write the next great novel right there in the cubicle. I flipped through one and found a doodle of a duck wearing a monocle. "Ah yes, clearly a masterpiece," I chuckled. "Forget Hemingway, I've got *Ducksworth the Distinguished* right here!"

Second drawer: stress balls. I counted eight. Eight stress balls, each one a testament to my struggle with Peter's endless budget meetings. "Who needs this many stress balls?" I asked aloud, and from the depths of the drawer, the office ghost of my past replied, "You did. And remember: stress balls don't work if you're throwing them at Peter."

Then came the infamous junk drawer the final frontier. It was full of expired gum, rubber bands, an old phone charger that didn't fit any of my current devices, and a single slipper. How I lost just one slipper in an office cubicle is still a mystery. Did I spontaneously turn into Cinderella during lunch breaks? I held it up like an artifact from a bygone era, muttering, "How did this even happen? Was there a foot race I wasn't invited to?"

By the time I packed up the last sticky note that read, "Fire Peter," I felt lighter. Each discarded paperclip, broken stapler, and half-empty Advil bottle represented years of hard work, caffeine-fueled triumphs, and suppressed rants. "You know what, past me? Thanks for all the memories," I said, tossing the sticky note like a confetti celebration. "And thanks for the motivation to start a petition against office snacks that taste like cardboard!"

As I stepped back to admire my now-empty desk, I realized I'd done it. I was free! No more awkward water cooler conversations about the weather or pretending to enjoy those terrible office donuts. "I'm like a butterfly emerging from a cocoon, if that cocoon was filled with paperclips and existential dread," I laughed.

With a final glance at my once-occupied desk, I walked away, feeling like I'd just broken up with a clingy ex. "You'll miss me when I'm gone," I called over my shoulder, "but I'll never have to share the remote again!"

SAYING GOODBYE

And then came the hardest part: saying goodbye to the people. It's funny how you don't realize how attached you get to your oddball coworkers until you're standing at the exit, cardboard box in hand, looking like a sitcom character who's just been written out of the show. These were the folks I'd spent years sharing desks, stale coffee, and more sarcastic comments than actual corporate reports. They'd seen me at my best, my worst, and that one holiday party incident involving too much eggnog and an ill-advised karaoke performance. It wasn't just leaving a job; it was leaving an entire ecosystem of quirks, personalities, and shared history.

Sophie from Marketing was the first to drop by. She was my partner-in-crime for terrible puns and quick comebacks, the one who could turn any meeting into a game of "Buzzword Bingo." She looked at me with mock horror. "Oh no! Who's going to keep me sane during conference calls?" she wailed, giving me a hug that felt more dramatic than a telenovela.

"You'll survive," I reassured her, patting her back. "Just make sure you keep up the snark. It's a tradition now."

She pulled back, grinning. "Who's going to send me those cat memes during budget meetings?" she asked, mock seriousness written all over her face.

"I'll still send them," I promised, laughing. "Retirement doesn't mean going offline. If anything, I'll have more time for memes now."

Sophie wiped away an imaginary tear. "Thank God. I couldn't live on dog memes alone. It's a cat-astrophe!"

Then came Jim from IT. Ah, Jim. The poor man had spent half his career trying to fix my never-ending tech disasters, from my "accidental" deletion of crucial project files to the "Help! The printer is trying to kill me!" moments. We'd bonded over the sheer absurdity of office technology.

"You're really leaving, huh?" Jim said, offering a fist bump because he was the coolest guy in the tech department.

I grinned. "Who's going to crash the system now?"

Jim chuckled. "Oh, I'm sure there's someone else around here who'll open three hundred tabs and bring the network to its knees. I'll just wait for the chaos!"

"I'll miss our conversations about 'the thingy that won't connect to the other thingy,'" he said, a mischievous twinkle in his eye.

I shook my head with a smile. "Hey, those were valid technical issues! One day I'll write a memoir titled *The Adventures of Thingy and Thingy!*"

And then, of course, there was Carl. Oh, Carl. We'd never really been close; our interactions were mostly limited to budget meetings where I'd mentally rewrite his entire presentation, wondering how someone could make numbers feel like a punishment.

He approached me with an overly firm handshake and a grin that was just a little too smug. "Guess you're leaving just when the budget's getting interesting," he said, his eyes glinting with the excitement of someone who believes spreadsheets are the key to happiness.

"Interesting isn't exactly the word I'd use," I replied, managing to suppress an eye roll. His handshake was unnecessarily firm, as if he were trying to win a grip-off. I could practically hear the "Rocky" theme music playing in the background.

As he walked away, I couldn't help but mutter under my breath, "Oh, Carl. The human teapot. Always steaming, never useful."

And that was it the last of the goodbyes. I felt a strange mixture of relief and heartache, like leaving a party just as the dessert tray arrived. These were the people who'd made the last 50 years a wild ride, from the golden years of my youth to the hilarious unpredictability of being a senior trying to retire all at once. What a journey indeed!

As I stepped outside, I took a deep breath and thought, "Well, here's to the next chapter! Let's just hope it comes with better snacks and fewer budget meetings!"

Chapter 2: Packing Up and Moving On

Selling a house is supposed to be one of the most stressful experiences in life, right up there with public speaking and accidentally hitting "reply all." So imagine my surprise when the house sold in two days. Two days! I was expecting to spend weeks cleaning up, dealing with nosy neighbors disguised as "potential buyers," and hiding the suspicious stain on the living room carpet let's just say it was a "vintage" design. Instead, it was a whirlwind of contracts, signatures, and frantic Googling of Delaware neighborhoods. Because nothing screams "I'm an adult!" like moving to a place you've never seen while hoping to find a decent pizza joint.

The real panic set in when I realized I actually had to pack everything up 50 years of accumulated treasures, memories, and more junk than an episode of *Hoarders*. I stood in the living room, staring at a mountain of boxes, feeling like I was about to compete in the Olympics of Cardboard Tetris. "Okay, focus," I thought, "how do I maximize space without giving up my collection of coffee mugs shaped like animals?"

I opened the first box, and out came a parade of mismatched socks, half-burnt candles, and what I can only assume was a relic from the '70s a lava lamp that hadn't been plugged in since Nixon was president. "This'll make a great conversation starter at my new place," I mused, as I carefully tucked it back into the box, wondering if I could start a new trend in interior decorating called "Vintage Disaster."

Next up was the kitchen. I opened a drawer to find an entire civilization of kitchen gadgets that could only be described as "what on Earth was I thinking?" A banana slicer? A corn cob stripper? "I've never even eaten corn off the cob in my life!" I exclaimed. I began to feel like a contestant on a game show where the prize is a lifetime supply of useless kitchen tools. "What's behind door number one? A grapefruit spoon! And behind door number two? A spaghetti measurer! Just what every home needs!"

As I moved to the living room, I discovered my old VHS collection. "Who even owns a VCR anymore?" I wondered, holding up a copy of *Titanic* that had clearly seen better days. I could practically hear the movie yelling, "I'm still not over Jack!" But I couldn't just throw them away; they held memories of cozy movie nights and questionable fashion choices from the '90s. I sighed, tossing them into a box labeled "Nostalgia: Handle with Care."

By the time I got to the garage, it was like stepping into a time capsule. Old bikes with flat tires, paint cans from projects I never finished, and oh look! an inflatable pool that hadn't seen water since the Great Drought of 2005. "I was going to throw a party, I swear!" I shouted to no one in particular. "Next year's a better year for swimming, right?"

The grand finale came when I opened the attic. "Why did I think storing holiday decorations was a good idea?" I gasped as a mountain of tinsel and half-deflated inflatable Santas greeted me. "I don't even celebrate Christmas! Who am I, the hoarder of holiday cheer?"

As I stuffed the last box, I felt like a contestant who had finally conquered the Tetris board. I stood back, surveyed the mountain of packed boxes, and couldn't help but chuckle. "Well, at least I won't be needing those packing peanuts," I said, tossing a handful in the air like confetti. "Goodbye, old house! Thanks for all the memories and questionable life choices. Now, let's see what Delaware has to offer hopefully a place with a much smaller lava lamp collection!"

THE PACKING CHAOS BEGINS

Packing is an art form, one I have yet to master. I tried to be organized, labeling boxes as "Kitchen Essentials," "Bathroom Supplies," and "Miscellaneous Crap I'll Never Use but Can't Bear to Throw Away." By the third box, however, it all blurred together, and soon I was shoving spatulas in with spare socks and old Christmas cards. "Nothing says 'I'm ready for a fresh start' like a box of spatula-sock hybrids," I muttered to myself.

Somewhere along the way, my dog, Murphy, decided that packing tape was his new favorite chew toy, turning each sealed box into a slobbery masterpiece. I looked over to see him proudly gnawing on a roll like it was the finest bone money could buy. "Great, Murphy. Now I have to worry about losing my tape and getting stuck with boxes that are practically begging for a visit from the tape police!"

As I struggled to fit an oversized lamp into a too-small box (because why buy the right size when you can just try to defy physics?), Murphy watched, clearly judging me. He lay sprawled on the floor, probably thinking, If only she applied this much effort to learning how to open my treat jar. "One day, Murphy, one day," I sighed, wrestling with the lamp like it was a stubborn octopus.

Meanwhile, the neighborhood cats seemed to hold an impromptu meeting in our driveway, watching me stumble over bubble wrap like they were critiquing my performance. "What is this amateur hour?" I could've sworn one of them shook its head in disapproval, as if to say, "You call that a packing technique?"

Every time I popped a piece of bubble wrap, they perked up, eyes wide with a mix of horror and fascination, as if I was performing some sort of tragic comedy. "Look at her! She's not even double-taping!" one of them whispered to another, and I could almost hear the condescending feline snickers. "Someone get the popcorn!"

In a moment of frustration, I turned to Murphy (Havanese malt).and shouted, "Why don't you help me, buddy? You're supposed to be my sidekick!" Murphy merely rolled onto his back, paws in the air, as if to say, "You're on your own, human. I'm off-duty."

As I attempted to stuff a pile of mismatched kitchen utensils into yet another box, a spatula flew out like a Frisbee, narrowly missing the gathering cats.

"Sorry, guys! Just a little kitchen chaos over here!" I laughed nervously, hoping they wouldn't file a complaint with the HOA.

Finally, after what felt like a marathon of packing madness, I took a step back to survey my work. Boxes were stacked haphazardly, tape was everywhere, and Murphy had commandeered a piece of bubble wrap as his new throne. "Well, I may not have mastered packing," I declared, "but at least I've achieved maximum chaos!"

As I waved goodbye to the driveway critics, I promised myself that the next time I moved, I'd hire a professional. Or maybe I'd just let Murphy and the neighborhood cats take charge. "At least they'd have a vision," I chuckled, "even if it's a vision of turning my house into a cat paradise."

THE DOG-RELATED TRAVEL ADVENTURES

The big moving day arrived, and so did Murphy's first road trip. Now, Murphy is usually a calm, collected dog until you put him in a car. The moment he hopped into the back seat, he transformed from a laid-back Hava Malt into a hyperactive toddler who just discovered Pixy Stix. He bounced from one window to the next, smudging the glass with nose prints while barking at every passing truck like they owed him money. "I'm not sure what you think you're gonna do,

Murphy," I laughed, "but last I checked, those trucks are not stopping for a doggy negotiation!"

Halfway through the journey, Murphy discovered that he could climb into the front seat. He promptly wedged himself between me and the steering wheel, turning the drive into a high-stakes game of "Avoid the Dog and Stay on the Road." Every time I tried to change lanes, he'd look up at me with those big, innocent eyes, as if to say, "What's wrong? I thought we were playing 'squeeze the driver!'" His attempts to navigate by licking my ear were not helpful. "Buster, I love you, but Delaware does not require dog-licking licenses for drivers!" I exclaimed, trying to swat him away like a pesky fly.

At one point, we pulled into a rest stop, and Murphy sprinted out like a canine version of Usain Bolt. There I was, chasing him through a grassy field, flailing my arms like a madwoman while fellow travelers looked on, probably wondering if this was some new exercise craze called "Catch Your Dog Before He Catches a Squirrel." "I swear this isn't part of the plan!" I yelled, hoping they didn't think I was trying to launch a new reality show called *Survivor: Dog Edition.*

Murphy was darting around with the speed of a caffeinated cheetah, weaving through unsuspecting picnickers like he was training for the Olympics. "Come back!" I shouted, as he zigzagged past a family eating sandwiches. They looked at me with a mix of sympathy and amusement, probably thinking, "That poor woman really thought she could outrun a dog who thinks he's in a high-speed chase!"

Finally, after what felt like an eternity, Murphy returned, panting and with his tail wagging furiously, as if to say, "See? I just needed to stretch my legs! What's the problem?" He dropped a stick at my feet like it was the trophy for winning the grand prize in "Best Dog of the Day." I couldn't help but laugh, despite the fact that I'd just burned off about 200 calories in a futile attempt to catch him.

As we got back into the car, I turned to him and said, "You know, Murphy, if this is how our road trips are going to go, I might just invest in a dog seatbelt. For my safety and yours." He just tilted his head, looking at me as if to say, "That sounds boring. Let's go chase more trucks!"

With that thought, I buckled up and braced myself for the next leg of the journey, wondering how many more spontaneous dog adventures lay ahead. "Just remember, buddy," I warned, "you're not the one with the steering wheel, and I don't come with a return policy!"

First Impressions of Delaware

Arriving in Delaware felt like stepping into an alternate reality one with fewer toll booths, shockingly more cows, and what appeared to be a competitive obsession with crab cakes. The "Welcome to Delaware" sign was barely in my rearview mirror when I was bombarded with five consecutive billboards, each advertising the "Best Crab Cakes in the State!" One of them actually dared to call out the others with a sassy, "Don't be crabby, ours are the real deal!" Clearly, Delaware took its seafood (and petty rivalries) seriously. I thought, if this is how Delaware lures people in, I might just be okay with it.

As I pulled up to the new house, a mix of excitement, exhaustion, and the desperate need for caffeine hit me all at once. The house was charming, I'll give it that like something out of a rom-com where the protagonist falls in love and discovers the magic of small-town living. Except here, the "Welcome" mat was so crooked it looked like it had been set down during an earthquake. It seemed to be whispering, *We're glad you're here, but good luck keeping your life in order.* Murphy, my four-legged partner in crime, sniffed around with the enthusiasm of a detective on his first big case, giving the front yard a thorough investigation before deciding it was time to leave his first official Delaware "present" right near the hydrangeas. Classy.

Midway through my struggle to wrangle a suitcase from the car (why do they always weigh twice as much as they did when you packed them?), a neighbor appeared like an NPC in a video game. She had the enthusiastic energy of someone who'd already baked something hopefully cookies. "Welcome to the neighborhood!" she chirped, her smile so wide I could practically see her molars. She handed me a plate of what looked like baked goods, but could also have been artisanal doorstops for all I knew.

"We're all a bit quirky here," she said with a wink, "but we don't bite."

I grinned, despite feeling like I was in a live-action episode of *The Twilight Zone*. "That's good to know," I replied, gesturing toward Murphy, who was now engaged in an epic battle with a clump of grass. "I brought my own weirdo."

She laughed, an actual belly laugh that made me wonder if she was laughing at the situation or if she was just one stubbed toe away from a breakdown. "Oh, we've got plenty of those. Just be careful of Charlie down the street. He still thinks Elvis is hiding in his attic."

"Does Elvis know?" I asked.

She doubled over, slapping her thigh like we were in some kind of country comedy sketch. "I sure hope so! We've heard some *suspicious* guitar riffs late at night."

As she sauntered off, I looked down at the cookies or at least, what I hoped were cookies and muttered, "Well, Murphy, it's either going to be baked goods or a sugar-coated brick. Wish me luck." Murphy, ever the optimist, wagged his tail and then immediately resumed digging a hole large enough to smuggle himself back to wherever we came from.

That first night was a symphony of chaos. I sat in the middle of half-unpacked boxes, staring at what was left of my rug Murphy had already gnawed one corner like it was a steak. He was now sprawled out in a way that only dogs can manage, snoring loud enough to shake the foundation. Meanwhile, I was trying to figure out how one person could accumulate so much *stuff* and still never find the one thing they needed like a decent wine opener. I grabbed a screwdriver and decided that desperate times called for desperate measures.

As I sipped my crudely opened wine (from a coffee mug because, apparently, glasses were a luxury I hadn't unpacked yet), it hit me. Moving isn't just about packing boxes and surviving cross-state road trips with a dog who thinks grass is an enemy combatant. It's about the unexpected adventures, the neighbors with bizarre conspiracy theories, and the crooked welcome mats that somehow feel like home.

I had no clue what Delaware had in store for me, but I was pretty sure it involved more crab cakes, a few run-ins with Elvis (or Charlie), and a whole lot of laughing at how hilariously unprepared I was for this new chapter. One thing was for sure: it was going to be a ride so funny, I might just laugh my way through the entire state.

Chapter 3: Settling In: Unpacking a Journey Through Chaos

I always thought unpacking would be easier than packing. After all, the boxes are labeled, right? WRONG. Somewhere between "Bathroom Essentials" and "Random Stuff I Couldn't Fit Anywhere Else," it became clear that the labels were more like optimistic lies, crafted by someone who clearly hadn't unpacked their own boxes in years. Who knew I'd need a PhD in deciphering my own handwriting to figure out why I put one slipper, a spatula, and a Halloween mask in the same box? Was I preparing for a costume party in the kitchen?

Day One of Settling In: The Coffee Quest

Day one of settling in started with a simple goal: find the coffee maker. Seemed straightforward enough. I could almost smell the rich aroma wafting through my new kitchen. But after opening 14 boxes only to discover things like expired spices, a rogue Monopoly piece, and Murphy's collection of stolen socks I began to lose hope. "Who needs caffeine when you have pure confusion?" I muttered, desperately trying to recall if drinking hot water with a cinnamon stick qualified as tea. Spoiler: it does not.

Murphy, meanwhile, was having the time of his life. Every opened box was a new adventure. He dove headfirst into a pile of bubble wrap and emerged looking like a dog-shaped astronaut. "Houston, we have a good boy," I announced as he proudly paraded around in his crinkly new outfit, sending bits of bubble wrap flying everywhere. It was like a party had broken out in the living room, and I was merely the unwilling chaperone.

After hours of rummaging through boxes, I finally found the coffee maker… nestled between a bread knife and a throw pillow. Because of course that's where it would be. My mind raced as I opened the cabinet above the sink, praying to the caffeine gods that I wouldn't have to face another coffee-related tragedy. When I couldn't find the coffee filters, I briefly considered using a paper towel. But after envisioning a coffee-related house fire on my first day, I settled for a Diet Coke instead. Breakfast of champions.

THE SHOWER CURTAIN SAGA

When it comes to moving, there's always that one essential item you forget, and in my case, it was a shower curtain. The first morning, I optimistically turned on the water, thinking, *How bad could it be?* I soon discovered that taking a shower without a curtain is less like bathing and more like re-enacting the opening scene of *Titanic,* complete with water gushing everywhere and me slipping around, yelling, "I'll never let go!"

Desperate times called for desperate measures. I found an old bed sheet, tied it to the curtain rod with hair ties, and voila! Makeshift curtain in place. Standing back to admire my handiwork, I thought, "Martha Stewart, eat your heart out." Of course, halfway through my shower, the sheet gave up on life and fell with the grace of a fainting goat. Murphy, sensing my struggle, poked his head in to watch me wrestle with a soggy sheet like a gladiator. "Thanks for the emotional support, buddy," I grumbled, slipping on a puddle and almost taking him down with me.

By the end of it, the bathroom looked like a crime scene, the victim being "personal dignity." I mopped up the carnage with a hand towel because, naturally, the real towels were still buried somewhere in a box labeled "BATH MAYBE?" It was a sobering moment that made me wonder why I'd ever thought moving would be a smooth transition.

MAKING NEW FRIENDS... SORT OF

Meeting new people is always awkward, but meeting new neighbors is an Olympic event in social discomfort. Determined to make a good impression, I ventured outside with a batch of store-bought cookies. You know, just a little "Hi, I'm the new person" gesture. My first stop was the house two doors down, where a man in a "World's Greatest Elvis Fan" T-shirt answered the door. This had to be Charlie

"Hey there! I'm new to the neighborhood," I said, holding out the cookies like a peace offering. "Just wanted to introduce myself."

Charlie squinted at the cookies like they might be poisoned. "These aren't peanut butter, are they? I've got a dog who's allergic to everything except beef jerky."

"Oh, uh, no! Just chocolate chip."

He nodded slowly, then whispered, "I saw your dog sniffin' around. He seems... capable." Capable of what? Taking down a squirrel mafia? I smiled awkwardly, said my goodbyes, and made a mental note to keep Murphy far, far away from Greg's house.

My next attempt at socializing was at the neighborhood park. I figured taking Murphy out for a walk would be a great way to meet people. What I hadn't anticipated was that Murphy would see this as an opportunity to mark every single tree in Delaware. Every. Single. One. It was like watching an artist paint a masterpiece in slow motion, except instead of brushes, he was using… well, you get the idea.

Just as I was dragging him away from his 84th tree stop, a fellow dog owner approached with a friendly smile. "What kind of dog is he?" she asked, as Murphy attempted to climb into her lap.

"Oh, he's a Hava Malt -slash-personal-chaos-generator," I joked, prying him off her.

She laughed. "That's nothing. Mine ate my car keys last week. Had to wait two days to get them back, if you know what I mean."

I nodded, silently vowing to never borrow her car. Because nothing says friendship like a dog that eats your means of transportation.

Unpacking Roulette

Back at home, the unpacking process had turned into a game I liked to call "Unpacking Roulette." Would I open a box of dishes? Towels? Or my collection of novelty socks? Nobody knew! It was a thrill ride, except without the thrill just a lot of guessing and occasional swearing.

After finally finding the toaster (in a box marked "BEDROOM ESSENTIALS"), I rewarded myself with a piece of toast and a dance break. Murphy joined in by chasing his tail, proving that even in the middle of moving chaos, there's always time for joy. Or insanity. It's a thin line.

Just as I was getting into a groove, I opened a box labeled "FRAGILE" only to find... the lava lamp. Ah yes, I thought, the one item guaranteed to make me question every life choice. I plugged it in, half-expecting it to explode, but it flickered to life, glowing like a beacon of poor taste. "Congratulations," I muttered to myself. "You've officially brought the 70s back to life."

Home Is Where the Weird Is

The first night in the new house felt oddly cozy, despite the chaos. I sat on the couch (which was still wrapped in plastic), sipping wine from a coffee mug, and watching Murphy chase a rogue moth across the living room. It wasn't perfect, but it was home-ish.

Just as I was about to drift off, I heard a familiar sound outside: a faint guitar riff. I froze. Was it Charlie? Or Elvis?!

"Guess we'll find out," I whispered to Murphy, who wagged his tail in agreement, clearly ready for whatever shenanigans were about to unfold.

And with that, I turned off the lava lamp and settled in, knowing that life in Delaware was going to be one wild ride full of unexpected encounters, awkward moments, and, if I was lucky, the occasional good crab cake.

At least now, I had a dog by my side, a house filled with half-unpacked boxes, and neighbors who believed in Elvis sightings. And really, what more could a person ask for?

Well... maybe just one thing: a properly installed shower curtain.

THE UNEXPECTED GUESTS

The next day, as I was slowly coming to terms with my new life, I heard a knock at the door. This could only mean one thing: *unexpected guests*. I took a deep breath, tucked my hair into a bun that might've been stylish if it hadn't been formed in a hurry, and opened the door.

Standing there was a woman in her forties, holding a casserole dish that looked suspiciously like it had been lifted straight out of a 1950s cookbook. "Hi! I'm Diane from across the street!" she said, beaming. "Welcome to the neighborhood! I brought you some lasagna."

I was momentarily speechless. "Um, thanks! This is... unexpected!"

"Oh, honey, it's a tradition around here. You move in, you get lasagna. It's practically law," she said, smiling as if she were passing down ancient knowledge.

Murphy took that moment to escape my grasp and sprint out the door, his nose leading him straight to Diane's feet. "And that's Murphy," I said, slightly panicking. "He's just checking you out. He's very friendly... well, more like chaotic."

Diane chuckled as she bent down to pet him. "I can see! I love dogs! He looks like a sweet boy."

As Murphy proceeded to sniff the casserole with the seriousness of a fine wine connoisseur, I wondered if I should be more concerned about his judgmental nose or the fact that he was actively contemplating stealing dinner. "Um, I assure you, he's never stolen anything… yet," I said, trying to sound convincing.

Diane laughed heartily, and in that moment, I realized: maybe making friends in this new place wouldn't be so terrifying after all.

"Come on in! I'll get you a plate," I said, feeling a surge of confidence. I wasn't ready for company, but maybe some lasagna and a chat with my new neighbor would make this house feel more like home.

As we sat at the kitchen table with Murphy snoozing happily at my feet, I thought about how sometimes the best parts of settling in weren't just about the boxes or the furniture. It was about the people who welcomed you in, ready to share their stories, laughter, and yes, even their lasagna

Chapter 4: The Quest for Friendship

Making friends as an adult is a little like dating, but without the wine to dull the awkwardness. In New York, friendships came naturally half the time, you'd meet people by yelling at the same pigeon or bonding over the misery of the subway. Seriously, you could walk into a coffee shop and accidentally lock eyes with a fellow caffeine addict, and suddenly you're sharing your life story while lamenting how the barista thinks "medium" is an acceptable size.

But in Delaware? It's a whole different ballgame. And by "ballgame," I mean "a series of social encounters where no one knows what inning they're in, and everyone's afraid to make the first pitch." It's like attending a game where the crowd is silently judging you for even showing up in a T-shirt that isn't plaid. You're standing there, clutching your snack like it's a life preserver, wondering if the hot dogs come with a side of small talk or if you have to earn that privilege.

Let's talk about that local coffee shop. In New York, you could walk in, overhear someone passionately arguing that the pumpkin spice latte is a basic crime against humanity, and join in without a second thought. But in Delaware, the baristas look at you like you just asked for a triple shot of unicorn tears. The most thrilling thing I overheard was two women discussing their latest victories in lawn maintenance "Did you see my azaleas? They've finally bloomed!" I tried to jump in with, "Are they thriving like my Netflix binge-watching habits?" But they just blinked at me as if I'd recited the alphabet backwards.

And then there's the small talk. In New York, your opening line could lead to a debate about whether a hot dog is a sandwich or if it's just a poor excuse for a taco. In Delaware, the barometer of good conversation seems to revolve around the best mulch for gardens. I once tried to throw in a comment about the weather being too nice for winter, and they all nodded like I'd just quoted the Bible. Meanwhile, I felt like I was the awkward kid at a school dance, standing by the punch bowl, contemplating whether I should just dump it on my head to make a grand exit.

The neighborhood BBQs were no different. In New York, the host would greet you with, "Grab a burger, and for the love of God, don't touch the kale!" But here? I was handed a plate with a lukewarm hot dog, a side of potato salad that looked suspiciously like it had gone to college and dropped out, and a group of people discussing the merits of slow-cooked brisket like it was an Olympic event. Trying to break into these tightly-knit clusters felt like I was crashing a family reunion where everyone had brought their favorite embarrassing stories about that one cousin who still thinks wearing socks with sandals is a fashion statement.

"Hey, have you tried the homemade pickles?" one woman asked, and I nodded, pretending to be as excited about pickles as I was about a root canal. The conversation quickly shifted to her recent trip to the farmer's market, and while I wanted to ask if they sold anything more exciting than kale, I just smiled and listened, wondering if I could make a getaway without anyone noticing.

At one point, someone mentioned the annual "Crab Cake Cook-Off," and you'd think they'd just announced the apocalypse. "Did you hear about Betty?" someone gasped. "She used shrimp instead of crab!" I half-expected someone to faint from the shock. Meanwhile, I'm over here thinking, "Can we just agree that shrimp is like crab's less successful cousin?"

So here I was, navigating a social landscape where the most scandalous topic of conversation was whether it was appropriate to add mayonnaise to a crab cake. It felt like I was living in a sitcom where I was the clueless character thrown into the mix for comic relief, and everyone else had already memorized their lines. I thought, "If I can survive subway delays and the occasional pigeon attack, surely I can survive this," but each awkward encounter left me more convinced that making friends in Delaware was a quest worthy of a medieval epic, complete with dragons, valiant knights, and an endless supply of potato salad.

As I embarked on this friendship quest, I reminded myself that maybe this was just the beginning. If I could master the intricacies of the New York social scene, I could surely conquer the laid-back approach of Delawareans. I just needed to find my tribe preferably one that didn't hold "The Great Pickle Debate" as their main topic of interest. It was going to take time, patience, and maybe a few more hot dogs before I'd finally fit in, but I was ready to step up to the plate hopefully without dropping my food on anyone's shoes this time!

THE POTLUCK PERILS

I kicked off my quest at the local "Meet the Neighbors" community gathering a potluck event that promised food, fun, and "a chance to make lifelong connections." Spoiler alert: Lifelong connections may vary. Determined to impress, I decided to go big. I spent an entire afternoon making deviled eggs, which I discovered is the culinary equivalent of babysitting a toddler with glue sticks chaotic and far messier than expected. By the time I finished, I had yolk in my hair, mustard on the ceiling, and exactly four eggs that survived the journey intact. Not exactly Martha Stewart, but good enough.

As I entered the event, I walked in with my plate of eggs and a please-like-me smile, scanning the crowd. It was a sea of unfamiliar faces, all engaged in lively discussions about... what? Gardening? Composting? Elvis sightings? I felt a wave of panic wash over me as I spotted a group gathered around a bowl of mystery punch. Mustering my courage, I sidled up to them and introduced myself.

"Hi, I'm new here!" I said, as one egg slid off the plate and landed yolk-side down on the ground. The group stared at me like I'd just unleashed a rabid raccoon. One guy muttered, "That feels symbolic."

Trying to recover, I casually asked, "So... how's everyone feeling about Elvis sightings these days?" The silence was deafening. Oh God, I thought, they're not Charlie's people. Abort!

AWKWARD ENCOUNTERS

The night continued in much the same fashion. Every conversation felt like stepping on a rake awkward, painful, and immediately regrettable. I approached one woman, hoping to find common ground. "You know," I said, "I've always wanted to learn how to garden."

"Oh, we don't garden," she replied with a straight face. "We compost."

"Compost. Right. That's... totally different," I stammered. I tried to pivot with a joke. "Is composting just gardening but with commitment issues?"

She blinked slowly and took a sip of her punch. I made a mental note: Don't joke about composting. These people take their rotten vegetables seriously.

In a last-ditch effort, I approached another group that was huddled around a bowl of something that suspiciously resembled gelatinous green sludge. "What's this?" I asked, gesturing at the bowl.

"Oh, that's our famous seaweed salad!" one woman beamed, as if she were presenting a trophy.

"Seaweed salad, huh? So... this is what we're eating instead of, like, actual food?" I replied, trying to mask my horror with enthusiasm.

They laughed, clearly unaware of my inner turmoil. "You get used to it!" one of them said. "It's good for you!"

Great, I thought. The road to friendship is paved with seaweed and unspoken regrets.

Friendships in New York vs. Delaware: A Study in Contrasts

In New York, your best friend is whoever happens to be standing next to you when your metro card stops working. Friendships are fast, intense, and forged in the fires of mutual suffering. But Delaware? Friendships here are like slow-cooked brisket: they take time, patience, and the right amount of seasoning (which I assume means complimenting people's recycling bins).

I tried to blend in by adopting some local habits. I peppered my conversations with "y'all," but it sounded less "friendly neighbor" and more like a tired parrot. I also learned the hard way that Delawareans take their crab cakes more seriously than their taxes. When I casually mentioned that I prefer lobster rolls, three people gasped, and one woman clutched her pearls like I'd just insulted her grandmother.

"Lobster rolls? In this house?!" she exclaimed, as if I'd committed a heinous crime against seafood.

"No, no, I didn't mean to offend! I just thought they were, you know, delicious!" I babbled, desperately trying to backpedal as she stared me down like I was wearing a lobster roll costume.

Making the Rounds

By the end of the night, I realized making friends was going to take a bit more effort than showing up with eggs. I found myself standing by the punch bowl, trying to look busy and pretending to enjoy the seaweed salad when I noticed Charlie, the Elvis fanatic, across the room. He was deep in conversation, gesturing dramatically like he was auditioning for a role in a Broadway musical.

I decided to approach him, hoping for a lifeline. "Hey, Charlie! What's the scoop on Elvis's sightings these days?" I asked, trying to channel my best impression of casual interest.

"Oh, it's been quiet lately," he replied, leaning in as if sharing a state secret. "But I heard he's been spotted at the diner down the road."

"Really? Is that the one with the killer milkshakes?" I asked, trying to find some common ground.

He nodded vigorously. "Best in the state! You should definitely check it out. Just be careful. There's been talk of a squirrel gang running wild."

"Squirrel gang?" I chuckled, half convinced he was joking. But the intensity in his eyes told me he was 100% serious. "Noted! I'll steer clear of any squirrel-related incidents."

Charlie grinned, and for the first time, I felt like maybe, just maybe, I had made a connection.

THE GREAT "WELCOME TO THE NEIGHBORHOOD" GIFT

As I left the potluck, the host handed me a mason jar filled with something that looked suspiciously like pickled beets.

"Welcome to the neighborhood," she said with a smile that was equal parts friendly and unnerving.

"Thanks! I love... um, jars," I lied, accepting the jar like it was a live grenade.

Driving home, I held the jar up to the light, examining the contents. "Well, at least I can say I have my first neighborly gift!" I declared to Murphy, who was happily snoring in the passenger seat.

As I parked the car, I decided to give the pickled beets a try. "Why not? It's an adventure!" I thought, bravely unscrewing the lid. A pungent aroma wafted out, and I nearly gagged. "Okay, maybe not an adventure for today."

Murphy's Role in the Quest

The next day, I decided to take Murphy out for a walk, hoping the fresh air would clear my head and possibly lead to more neighborly encounters. As we strolled down the street, I noticed a woman with a dog on the opposite side. I waved enthusiastically, determined to make a new friend.

"Hey there! Nice dog!" I called out, trying to sound as cheerful as a golden retriever.

"Thanks! What kind is yours?" she replied, her smile warm and inviting.

"Oh, he's... well, let's just say he keeps me on my toes," I said, as Murphy darted around my legs, tangling me in his leash like an overzealous puppeteer.

She chuckled, which felt like a good sign. "That's nothing! Mine ate my car keys last week. Had to wait two days to get them back, if you know what I mean."

I grimaced. "Two days? You must have the patience of a saint. I would've needed therapy for that."

She laughed, holding up her hands. "Trust me, I'm still recovering. Every time I see those keys, I can't decide whether to use them or bury them in the yard."

I shook my head in mock horror. "I don't know if I should introduce Murphy to that level of mischief. He's already halfway there!"

"Want to do a playdate sometime?" she asked, glancing at Murphy, who was now hopping around like a kangaroo auditioning for the circus.

"Absolutely!" I replied, feeling a spark of hope. "I think Murphy would love it."

As we exchanged numbers, I realized that maybe, just maybe, I was making progress in my quest for friendship.

THE QUEST CONTINUES

Back at home, the unpacking process had devolved into a game I liked to call "Unpacking Roulette." Would I open a box of dishes? Towels? Or my collection of novelty socks? Nobody knew! It was a thrill ride, except without the thrill just a lot of guessing and occasional swearing.

I opened a box labeled "FRAGILE" only to find... the lava lamp. Ah yes, I thought, the one item guaranteed to make me question every life choice. I plugged it in, half-expecting it to explode, but it flickered to life, glowing like a beacon of poor taste. "Congratulations," I muttered to myself. "You've officially brought the 70s back to life."

Just as I was getting into a groove, my phone buzzed with a text. It was the woman from the park! "Let's set up a playdate for the dogs! How's Saturday?"

"Saturday sounds great! Can't wait!" I replied, my heart racing with excitement.

THE FIRST PLAYDATE

Saturday arrived, and I was a bundle of nerves. What if Murphy embarrassed me? What if I embarrassed myself? What if we both ended up running away from the social scene, never to be seen again?

As I approached the park, I spotted her Lauren throwing a frisbee for her dog, a ridiculously energetic Golden Retriever named Buddy. Murphy, on the other hand, was more interested in sniffing every blade of grass as if it contained the secrets of the universe

Chapter 5: Embracing Change

The thing about menopause is that no one really warns you. One minute, you're coasting along, living your best life, feeling fabulous, like you've finally got it all figured out. And then bam! Your body decides to turn up the heat like it's been possessed by an angry furnace that's had one too many espressos. Welcome to *Menopause: The Musical*, featuring a soundtrack of your own exasperated sighs, starring night sweats, mood swings, and an overwhelming urge to slap anyone who dares ask if you're "okay." Spoiler alert: We are not okay, Todd. Get back in your lane.

The Heat Is On

Let's dive into the fiery depths of this experience. It begins with the infamous hot flashes, those moments when you feel like you've become the human equivalent of a volcano. One moment, you're sitting there sipping your chamomile tea, the next, your body decides it's auditioning for the role of "Most Dramatic Temperature Change." You can't even trust your own thermostat anymore.

You've got to carry a mini fan everywhere like it's your emotional support animal.

You know what really stings? Those moments when you're in a meeting or out to dinner, and suddenly you feel like you've been thrown into a sauna. You look around, trying to gauge if anyone else is feeling the same fiery wrath. "Is it just me, or did we all decide to crank the heat up to inferno?" You catch a glimpse of the poor guy across the table, slowly sinking into his chair like a melting ice cream cone. No one's safe from the menopausal meltdown.

And don't even get me started on the night sweats! Ah, the night sweats the cruel joke of your slumber. You go to bed, ready to cuddle up with a good book, and then it feels like your body has declared open season on your comfort. You wake up at 3 a.m., drenched in sweat like you just ran a marathon through the Sahara. Sheets clinging to you like an ex who refuses to take the hint. "Is this my life now? Am I a human sauna? Am I supposed to charge admission?"

And let's not forget those mid-sweat existential crises. You lie there, drenched in your own perspiration, thinking, "Was it the spicy curry I had for dinner, or is my body just throwing a rave?"

You're torn between longing for the cool breeze of a winter night and wondering how on Earth you ever thought it was a good idea to sleep with flannel sheets. "They said they were cozy!" you lament, feeling like a burrito wrapped in regret.

THE EMOTIONAL ROLLERCOASTER

Now, let's talk about mood swings, the emotional rollercoaster no one signed up for. You remember the days when your biggest stressor was figuring out what to watch on Netflix? Those days are long gone. Now, one minute you're fine, just casually sipping your tea and watching a squirrel do something cute outside. The next? You're crying uncontrollably because, oh my God, look at how that little squirrel is gathering acorns! He's just so organized, and why is life so beautiful and sad at the same time?!

The way I see it, squirrels are basically the furry versions of overachievers. "Look at me! I'm hoarding all my acorns! My life is together!" Meanwhile, you're contemplating whether you can really call it a "successful day" if you didn't wear pants until 4 p.m.

And speaking of squirrels, those adorable little creatures are suddenly everywhere especially when you're trying to keep it together. You're at the grocery store, and there's a display of nuts. "Oh no," you think, "not the nuts." One look at those nuts, and you're suddenly deep in a spiral of existential dread, wondering why you can't manage to keep your life as organized as that little squirrel's stash. "What kind of a friend am I? I might as well start a support group for the world's worst friend."

Then there are those moments when you find yourself in a heated debate with your husband over something utterly ridiculous like the proper way to load the dishwasher. One minute you're calmly explaining your method, and the next, you're ready to throw a plate at his head because he dared to suggest that the forks should go on the left instead of the right. "Why do you hate me, Todd?" And the poor man is just standing there, bewildered, like he just walked into the wrong movie. "I didn't even know I was on trial!"

You can practically hear the mood swing warning bells going off in your brain, but it's too late your inner rage monster is unleashed. "I can't help it! The dishwasher has a system, and you're ruining everything!" And then, just as quickly, you're weeping over the fact that your cat has chosen to ignore your attempts at affection. "Why won't you love me, Whiskers? Is it because I'm old now? I still have so much love to give!"

Wardrobe Malfunctions

And we can't talk about menopause without addressing the wardrobe malfunctions. Remember when your clothes used to fit? Pepperidge Farm remembers. I put on a pair of jeans the other day and suddenly felt like I was auditioning for *Cirque du Soleil*. There was jumping, lunging, and a full-on battle between my body and the fabric, and spoiler alert: the fabric won. Getting dressed now feels like preparing for combat.

I never thought I'd be the type to wear elasticated waistbands full-time, but here we are. Yoga pants are my new best friends, the stretchy, forgiving kind that allow me to breathe freely. I've embraced my inner sloth. Who needs the judgment of denim when you can swan around in comfort? But then again, as I rummage through my closet, I see all those lovely, stylish clothes that are now just mocking me. "Oh, remember when you wore us? Good times, right?"

But the best part? The unexpected surprise when you put on that "one-size-fits-all" dress that you haven't worn since your best friend's wedding.

You slip it on, and suddenly you're channeling a character from a low-budget horror film. "Is it a dress or a straightjacket? Who knows!" You stare in the mirror, trying to decide if you're going to rock the "I'm a sexy sausage" look or just admit defeat and go back to your trusty pajamas.

And let's not forget about bras. Those underwires are personal vendettas at this point. Every time I try to wear one, I hear it whisper, "We're done here, lady." I swear I'm ready to launch a nationwide campaign for the end of underwire. My "bra drawer" has officially become a graveyard for the undergarments of my past. You know it's bad when you find a bra that used to fit, only to hear it laugh in your face. "Ha! You thought you could wear me again? Good luck with that!"

THE GREAT UNDERWEAR DILEMMA

And speaking of underwear, what happened to the days when we could wear cute little knickers without a care? One day you're happily sporting your favourite pair, and the next, you feel like you've been stuffed into a sausage casing. I swear, my underwear looked me in the eye one morning and said, "We had a good run, but it's over." I now have two categories of underwear: "Will Make Me

Cry" and "Just in Case I Have to Go to the Emergency Room."

And don't even get me started on the endless cycle of panty shopping. You walk into the store, ready to browse, only to feel like you've stepped into a nightmare. "How many different types of underwear do we need?" You grab a handful, convinced that this time will be different, but then the moment you try them on, it's like they conspired against you. "Surprise! We're actually torture devices!"

LIGHT-HEARTED TIPS FOR SURVIVAL

So, here's my advice: embrace it. No, really. Get yourself a personal fan, keep ice packs in your freezer like they're a precious commodity, and stock up on chocolate like the apocalypse is coming. Because nothing says, "I'm handling my life" like a stash of emergency chocolate bars hidden in the vegetable crisper.

Oh, and never underestimate the power of a good laugh. When the mood swings hit hard, just remember that laughter is the best medicine except when you're experiencing hot flashes in public. Then, it's just awkward. "Why is that woman fanning herself while wearing a parka in July?" They'll have questions, and I'll have no answers.

And while you're at it, buy yourself a good supply of iced tea and that frozen yogurt that tastes like your childhood dreams. Nothing says "I'm going through menopause" like sitting on your couch with a pint of "I'm Not Sorry" ice cream. You've earned it, my friend.

Also, don't be afraid to tell someone, "No, I'm not okay, Todd, but thanks for asking," while simultaneously glaring at them so hard they feel it in their soul. That's a power move right there, folks. "I appreciate your concern, but I'm about two seconds away from setting my hair on fire. Now, if you'll excuse me, I need to go cool off before I throw a table over my emotional state."

Oh, and here's a pro tip: invest in a fun pillow. You know, the one with a cheeky saying on it? Mine says, "I'm not saying I'm old, but I remember when the Dead Sea was just sick." Every time I plop down, it reminds me to embrace the chaos. You have to find humour in the madness, or it'll eat you alive.

Conclusion: Finding the Joy in Chaos

So, let's raise our ice cream scoops to the wild ride that is menopause. It may not be pretty, and there will be moments when you wonder if you've completely lost the plot, but somewhere amidst the chaos, you'll discover the joy of being unapologetically you.

And as we all know, nothing brings people together like shared suffering. So let's laugh at the absurdity of it all. After all, in the grand journey of life, we're all just trying to navigate the wild world of menopause, one fan at a time.

Chapter 6: Asthmatic Love and Unstoppable Passion

Life post-hysterectomy wasn't all quesadilla philosophy and morphine-induced wisdom; there was also Greg, and things between us had taken on a whole new spark. One night, we were both curled up on the couch, watching some forgettable rom-com, when his hand found mine. It was an unspoken invitation, the kind that doesn't need words, and before I knew it, we were locked in a kiss that had no intention of stopping.

We made our way to the bedroom, shedding clothes like breadcrumbs along the way, and I felt that familiar heat between us. It was passionate, heady, the kind of night that makes the post-surgery aches and pains worth it. Greg's touch was electric, and I was completely lost in the moment, feeling that lovely rush you only get with someone who knows you so well.

Then, just as things got really intense, I felt the tightness start in my chest. My breath hitched not in the sexy, breathless way, but in the "lungs forgetting how to work" way. My trusty asthma kicked in right at the most inconvenient moment. My breathing sounded like the broken bellows of an old accordion, but I wasn't about to let it slow me down. I felt around the nightstand with a determination that probably could've moved mountains, finally grabbing my inhaler.

Taking a quick puff, I shot Greg a look over the inhaler, my eyes saying, "Let's keep going." He chuckled, a bit surprised and a bit impressed. "Are you sure?" he asked, with that little grin of his.

"Oh, I'm more than sure," I said with a wink, tossing the inhaler aside with all the drama of a romance novel heroine, and in that moment, it was like my life depended on that one release do or die. As Greg moved closer, my breath was coming in shaky, shallow waves, and I could barely get the words out, but I found myself whispering, pleading in the most shamelessly seductive way, "Please...don't stop. I want all of it."

He held nothing back, and every nerve in my body seemed to fire all at once. It was like I'd been holding my breath for days, weeks even, and with one final rush, we reached that edge together. In a perfect, synchronized exhale, we both finished, collapsing in a tangled mess of limbs, sweat, and satisfied sighs.

I wasn't the only one gasping. We lay there, panting, and he chuckled, his chest rising and falling beside mine, both of us fully spent and blissfully out of breath.

PEE-GASMS: A HIDDEN PERK OF HYSTERECTOMY

As I settled into life without a uterus, I discovered a delightful new twist to my recovery: orgasmic peeing. It wasn't in any of the pamphlets, but it was undoubtedly one of the most exciting post-surgery surprises. The first time it happened, I thought maybe I'd finally gone mad from too much pain medication. There I was, innocently sitting on the toilet, when suddenly, my bladder decided to treat me to a surprise finale. It was like my body was saying, "Sorry for all the crap I put you through. Here's a little something to make up for it." I returned to the living room, wearing a ridiculous grin, and Greg immediately noticed. "What happened in there? You look like you've just seen a miracle." "You have no idea," I replied, trying to play it cool. "Let's just say that peeing has become a spiritual experience." At first, he didn't believe me. But the evidence became clear over the next few days, as I started chugging water like a college kid at a kegger. "Isn't that your fifth bottle today?" he asked suspiciously. "Hydration is important," I replied, as if it were some noble cause. But the truth was, I was just eager for my next "bathroom break." Greg caught on eventually. "Are you seriously that excited to pee?" he asked one evening, with a mix of amusement and disbelief. "Hey, it's the simple pleasures in life," I shot back. "And if peeing can be orgasmic, who am I to complain?"

Every time I felt the urge, I'd saunter off to the bathroom with a secret smile. Not in a "nature's calling" sort of way, but more in a "let's get to the good part" vibe. I'd close the door, settle down, and let my body do the rest. And each time, it was like my bladder was throwing me a private party.

Greg was onto me now, his eyebrows creeping higher each time I got up for another glass of water. One evening, he couldn't hold back. "Another refill?" he asked, feigning innocence, though the glint in his eye was anything but. I shrugged, lifting my glass, trying to look casual. "What? I'm just keeping hydrated. Good for the skin."

"Uh-huh." He smirked. "And for everything else, apparently." I couldn't help but laugh, the secret already halfway out of the bag.

Later that night, as I returned from another round of "refreshment," Greg glanced up from his book, pretending to be completely absorbed. "So, is it like… a little spark or a full-blown fireworks show?" he asked, looking as innocent as he could manage.

I blushed but couldn't resist. "Let's just say it's like the perfect happy ending to every bathroom break." He chuckled, eyes gleaming with mischief.

"Well, now I know why you've been taking longer in there," he teased, pulling me close. I laughed, wrapping my arms around him, knowing full well that I'd never look at the bathroom the same way again.

We called it "Love, Surgery Edition," and every day added a new chapter. Greg, for instance, seemed to think the remote retrieving was negotiable, but I was ready with the "doctor's orders" line for nearly everything: cooking, dishes, reaching for anything above knee height. And if I said it with enough flair, Greg usually caved, muttering something about me being an "incurable diva."

One Saturday, as I stretched on the couch, watching him carry a laundry basket across the room, he stopped in front of me, arms full of clothes, and grinned.

"Don't even try it. I'm not folding everything while you 'recover,'" he said, adding finger quotes.

"Oh, I wouldn't dream of it," I said, doing my best to look pathetically helpless. "It's just… well, you're doing so well on your own. It's actually kind of impressive."

He laughed, but I could tell he was secretly enjoying it. This new, slightly sassy dynamic had us both on our toes. I mean, sure, he rolled his eyes every time I dramatically declared, "But I'm recovering, darling," but his grin always gave him away. And I'd catch him now and then, talking to Murphy about it when he thought I couldn't hear.

"She's milking this, Murph," he'd say. "But who are we kidding? We'll probably still be fetching things for her in six months."

The funniest part was, Murphy would bark, tail wagging, as if they were both part of the same reluctant-but-willing support team. And in a way, they were.

By the time I'd graduated from surgery recovery to what Greg called my "forever plan for excuses," we were practically pros at the routine. But underneath the lighthearted teasing and excuses, I knew how lucky I was. Every look, every joke, even the eye rolls they were all little reminders of why I'd fallen for him in the first place.

FALLING FOR FRAN: BURNT CHEESE AND BURNT INHALERS

Before all the medical chaos, my love story with Greg had been built on everyday moments awkward encounters, burnt dinners, and the kind of jokes that only two weirdos in love could appreciate.

One of the first moments I realized I was falling for Greg was during a particularly disastrous attempt at making grilled cheese. We were tipsy, trying to act like we had our lives together, but the kitchen quickly filled with smoke as our sandwich dreams went up in flames.

"Oh, great," I muttered, waving a dish towel at the smoke detector. "Romance level: zero."

But Greg just laughed, taking my hand. "If we can survive this, we can survive anything."

He wasn't wrong. Love wasn't about perfect meals or romantic sunsets; it was about sharing inhalers, laughing at burnt cheese, and finding the absurd joy in life's chaos. It was waking up next to someone who thought you were beautiful, even when you had bedhead and morning breath.

We even created a list of "Greg and Ruth's Rules of Love," which included gems like:

1. **Always have an inhaler within reach.**
2. **Burnt cheese is still cheese.**
3. **If one of us falls asleep during a movie, the other gets dibs on snacks.**

Recovery Wins and Ridiculous Excuses

Life after surgery wasn't without its challenges, but it did come with plenty of moments where I shamelessly milked the "I had surgery" excuse for everything.

"Can you grab me the remote?" I asked Greg, sprawled dramatically on the couch.

"It's right next to you," he pointed out, not moving an inch.

"Yes," I replied, clutching my abdomen with exaggerated pain. "But surgery, remember?"

He rolled his eyes but handed me the remote anyway. "You realize you can't use that excuse forever, right?"

"Forever is a long time," I shot back. "But at least until I'm cleared for heavy lifting. So, another two weeks, minimum."

Murphy, our dog, seemed to be in on the act, too. Whenever I struggled to get up, he'd start barking, as if to say, "Hey, remember she had surgery!"

Greg would shake his head, laughing. "You've even got the dog trained to be your accomplice."

"Team effort," I'd say, giving Murphy a high-five.

Chapter 7: Rediscovering Love

Falling in love in your 50s is a bit like riding a bike except the bike is a little rusty, the wheel's wobble, and you're not entirely sure if you remember how to brake. It's a thrilling experience, like a ride on a carnival rollercoaster that's just a tad too rickety for your comfort. You find yourself gripping the handlebars, teeth clenched, praying the seatbelt actually works. One moment, you're gliding through the pleasant breeze of hope, and the next, you hit a bump and wonder if you should have just stuck to walking. But when you do get the hang of it? Oh boy, is it exhilarating! You laugh, you scream, and there's a very real possibility you might throw your hands up in the air and just let go. If it all goes sideways, at least you can say you tried and you've got a great story for the grandkids!

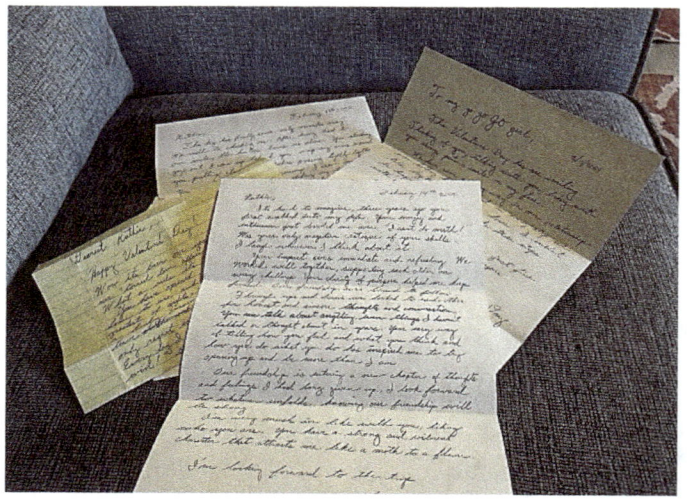

LOVE LETTERS AND SHARED INTERESTS

As things got more serious, Greg started sending me sweet little notes. He'd tape them to the fridge or leave them under my pillow. One read, "You're the best thing that's happened to me... next to the air fryer." Honestly, I couldn't even be mad. I do love that air fryer. It's practically a family member at this point.

Our shared interests weren't always conventional. We both had a strange obsession with watching infomercials at 2 a.m. and an unexplainable love for poorly made romantic comedies. One night, we watched a terrible rom-com where the lead character fell in love with a ghost. Halfway through, Greg turned to me and said, "If I ever die, please make sure I haunt you." I laughed and replied, "Deal! But only if you promise to knock stuff off the counters dramatically and say, 'Boo!' in a really cheesy voice."

REDISCOVERING LOVE: THE REAL-LIFE ROLLERCOASTER

Rediscovering love in midlife was nothing like the movies, and thank goodness for that. It was awkward, hilarious, and completely imperfect. There was no romantic montage with soft music playing in the background while we shared ice cream and slow-mo laughter over spilled milkshakes. It was more like a comedy sketch, filled with mishaps and miscommunication.

One weekend, we decided to cook dinner together a recipe from one of those fancy cooking shows where the chefs make everything look effortless. Let's just say our attempt at gourmet grilled cheese turned into a cheese explosion of epic proportions. We ended up laughing so hard that we forgot to set the timer, and by the time we remembered, our masterpiece was more charcoal than cheddar. But instead of being disappointed, we toasted our blackened sandwiches and declared,

"We're the new Gordon Ramsay, but with more laughter and less screaming!"

THE REAL TREASURES OF MIDLIFE ROMANCE

The truth is, love at this age comes with its own set of treasures ones you wouldn't have appreciated in your 20s. You find beauty in the mundane and joy in the absurd. It's about sharing those awkward moments, like when Greg attempted to dance in the living room to a song from my high school days, only to trip over his own feet and land on the sofa, which sent a decorative pillow flying across the room. We both burst into laughter, and for a moment, I thought, "This is love a little clumsy, a lot funny, and perfectly imperfect."

In a world where finding love can often feel like searching for a needle in a haystack, I was happily exploring the hay with Greg, knowing that every chuckle and shared look made the journey worth every wobble. Who needs a perfect bike when you can have a slightly rusty one that brings you laughter and love instead?

Conclusion: Love, Laughter, and the Air Fryer Chronicles

And if that love comes with air-fryer recipes and trivia night losses? Well, then I'm winning just like I would if I had won that trivia night, except now I have a great guy and an air fryer that makes dinner prep feel like a cooking show. It's the little things the quirky conversations, the shared glances that say "I get you," and the laughter that fills the gaps of our lives that make rediscovering love in your 50s a truly fantastic adventure. Here's to more messy dinners, spontaneous dance-offs, and late-night infomercial marathons. Who knew that love at this age could be so much fun?

Chapter 8: Adventures in Marriage

Breakfast Battles: The Culinary Showdown

Life with Greg has never been a picture-perfect fairy tale; it's more of a quirky sitcom where love and chaos collide in the kitchen. Our mornings often began with grand culinary ambitions that quickly devolved into slapstick comedy. One fine Saturday, I decided to channel my inner chef and create a breakfast extravaganza: a three-egg omelette loaded with spinach, feta, and all the spices I could find, which I assumed were culinary magic.

"Are you really doing this again?" Greg asked, raising an eyebrow like a concerned father watching his child attempt to climb a tree. "Last time, we nearly burned the house down."

I waved him off, flipping my hair like a culinary diva. "Pfft! Trust the process, my dear Watson!"

Just as I triumphantly served my masterpiece, Murphy, our over-enthusiastic Havanese malt golden retriever, decided it was a great time to audition for the role of "Kitchen Tornado." He launched himself onto the counter with the grace of a gazelle and promptly knocked over a cup of coffee, creating a brown tidal wave that threatened to engulf everything in its path.

"Murphy! No!" I shrieked, but the drama had already unfolded, and Greg was now performing a spectacular ballet as he attempted to navigate the sticky situation, only to slip and crash into the fridge.

"I've fallen, and I can't get up!" he groaned, looking more like a confused tortoise than a grown man.

"Looks like breakfast is off the menu!" I chuckled, offering him a hand, but the only thing I achieved was getting flour all over my face.

"Well, at least we won't starve! Flour-based, right?" he said, laughing despite himself as we surveyed the wreckage of our breakfast dreams.

Canine Chaos: The Great Dog Race

With breakfast a washout, we turned our attention to our two furry companions, Murphy and

HoneyBear. Walking them was like managing a circus act; one was a whirlwind of energy, while the other preferred to laze about like a queen on her throne.

One sunny Saturday, I thought, "This is going to be a peaceful stroll." Little did I know that peace was a luxury we couldn't afford. As soon as we stepped outside, Murphy took off like a rocket, dragging me behind him as if I were his own personal sled.

"Whoa! Slow down, Furball!" I yelled, grasping the leash like a lifeline, but he had other ideas, barking at a squirrel that seemed equally unamused by our antics.

Meanwhile, Greg strolled leisurely with HoneyBear, who was blissfully unaware of the chaos around her. "Want to swap?" he called out, chuckling at my predicament.

"Only if I get a non-shedding cat in return!" I retorted, trying to keep my balance while Murphy lunged after a particularly audacious squirrel.

After what felt like a marathon, I finally managed to reel in Murphy, panting and half-drenched in sweat. "Next time, you walk Murphy.

I'm just here for the snacks," I gasped, trying to regain my composure.

"Deal! But only if I can have the nachos," he said, grinning like the Cheshire Cat.

CHORE WARS: THE BATTLE OF THE BROOMS

Ah, chores the final frontier of married life. Greg and I had perfected the art of procrastination, turning household responsibilities into a theatrical performance that would make Shakespeare proud.

One weekend, we decided it was time to tackle the garage, which had become a black hole of forgotten treasures. "This is going to be our bonding moment," I declared, brandishing a broom like a sword.

"Bonding? I thought we were just going to get buried under an avalanche of junk!" he replied, eyeing the clutter like it might spring to life and attack.

"Let's see what treasures we uncover!" I said dramatically, pulling open a box marked "Holiday Decorations." A wave of glitter erupted from it like a New Year's Eve party gone wrong, covering us both.

"Great, now we're festive AND cleaning," Greg laughed, trying to shake off the sparkles like a dog after a bath.

As we delved deeper into the garage, we stumbled upon an old toy from Greg's childhood a half-deflated beach ball. "Remember this?" he said, holding it up like a prized possession.

"Of course! You used to say it was your best friend. I think it was just a reminder of your questionable sports skills!"

"Hey! I was very athletic! Just had a few off days… or years," he protested, puffing out his chest in mock pride.

As we laughed through the chaos, I realized that our shared insanity made us a team. We might not have tackled the garage, but we had created a new level of domestic bliss one that was equal parts absurdity and hilarity.

Date Night Adventures: The Quest for Culinary Delights

After a day filled with chaos and canine antics, we decided it was time for a proper date night. We had grand plans to explore a trendy new restaurant downtown, where the food promised to be as avant-garde as the décor, which was a fancy way of saying "prepare for the smallest portions imaginable."

As I dressed up, feeling like a million bucks, Greg emerged in his signature dinosaur T-shirt that read, "I'm just here for the food."

"Really?" I laughed, trying to suppress my giggles. "You're going to wear that?"

"Of course! It's a conversation starter!" he said, completely unfazed.

When we arrived at the restaurant, I couldn't help but notice the couple at the next table on what seemed like an awkward first date. The guy asked, "So, do you like... food?"

"Uh, yeah? I mean, who doesn't?" she replied, giggling nervously.

I leaned over to Greg and whispered, "Should we intervene? Like, 'Ask about their favorite cheese or don't mention exes!'"

"Let's leave them to their adventure. It's probably just as entertaining as ours!" he chuckled, digging into his dish, which was artfully arranged to resemble a modern art installation.

As we tried to decipher the menu, the waiter approached with our "deconstructed" dishes essentially just fancy words for regular food but with half the calories and three times the price. "And here we have the 'abstract interpretation of potatoes,'" I joked, picking up a plate with a single potato slice and a sprinkle of parsley. "I always wanted to eat art!"

"Now that's a diet plan I can get behind," Greg replied, mock-seriously.

After a night filled with laughter, bizarre bites, and a couple of side-eyes from the other diners, we finally stumbled home, feeling pleasantly stuffed with both food and love.

Laughing Through Life: Love in the Madness

As we collapsed onto the couch, exhausted but grinning from ear to ear, I reflected on our day. "You know, life with you is like a whimsical adventure full of unexpected plot twists and ridiculous characters," I mused, snuggling against him.

Greg grinned, wrapping his arm around me. "And you're the star of the show! Just remember to keep the breakfast chaos coming. We need more material for the next season."

"Deal! But I'm getting my revenge on that omelette tomorrow morning," I laughed, picturing the upcoming culinary catastrophe.

As we settled in for the night, I couldn't help but feel grateful for the unique madness that was our life together. We may not have mastered the art of adulthood, but our adventures both the absurd and the heartwarming were what made our marriage a one-of-a-kind masterpiece. And as I drifted off to sleep, I couldn't wait to see what delightful chaos awaited us in the morning.

Chapter 9: Embracing New Experiences

With retirement upon us, Greg and I decided it was time to embrace the kind of adventures we'd only dreamt about while stuck in the daily grind of our jobs. The days of mundane office meetings and deadlines were behind us, and now we were free to dive headfirst into life's quirky escapades. Who knew retirement could be this much fun?

As the first weeks of retirement rolled on, we quickly discovered that boredom had no place in our lives. We were determined to fill our days with laughter, spontaneity, and a healthy dose of ridiculousness. Our mantra? "Why not?"

The Great Retirement Adventure

Our first order of business was to tackle the world of hobbies. "Let's learn something new!" Greg suggested one afternoon, while we lounged on the couch surrounded by a sea of dog fur and leftover pizza.

"Like what? Competitive couch lounging?" I quipped, prodding him playfully. But he was undeterred.

"Why not pottery? It's therapeutic!" he exclaimed, his eyes sparkling with enthusiasm.

"Therapeutic? The last time I tried to 'become one with the clay,' I ended up with a lopsided ashtray that looked like a mutant pancake," I reminded him.

"Exactly! It'll be a fantastic story!" he replied, leaning back with a laugh. So, with that questionable logic firmly in place, we signed up for pottery classes.

THE CLAY CHRONICLES

Our first class was a whirlwind of excitement and chaos. The instructor, a no-nonsense woman named Greta, took one look at Greg eager face and probably wondered if she'd accidentally wandered into a comedy club instead of a ceramics studio.

"Alright, everyone, let's start with the basics," she said, demonstrating how to shape the clay. Greg always one to skip the boring part, jumped in without so much as a nod to the fundamentals.

Within minutes, he had clay everywhere on his face, in his hair, and somehow, on my glasses. "Look, Ruth! I'm making a masterpiece!" he declared, holding up what appeared to be a very confused lump of clay. It had more in common with a potato than a vase.

"Are you sure that's not an abstract representation of your last work meeting?" I laughed, reaching for my glasses to clear the smeared mess.

Greta was unperturbed. "Just remember, it's not about the end product; it's about the experience."

"Sounds like something you say to avoid bad reviews!" I shot back.

Culinary Capers

After a couple of weeks of shaping our very questionable pottery skills, we decided it was time to turn our attention to culinary arts. "Let's try cooking classes!" Greg suggested, bouncing with excitement.

"Sure! Because what could possibly go wrong in a room full of sharp knives and hot stoves?" I replied with mock seriousness.

The first class was a mishmash of chaos, laughter, and unintentional food disasters. Greg convinced he could channel his inner Gordon Ramsay, attempted to flambé a dish and ended up setting off the fire alarm instead. "Who knew sautéing could lead to a five-alarm situation?" I teased, waving away the smoke.

The instructor, a patient woman named Linda, tried to maintain order as we all coughed and giggled. "Just remember, cooking is all about trial and error!" she said, as I expertly set my apron on fire while attempting to stir a pot of what was supposed to be pasta but resembled an alien life form.

ROAD TRIP RUCKUS

Next, we decided it was time for a spontaneous road trip. "Let's hit the open road! Feel the wind in our hair!" Greg proclaimed, wearing his "Life is Good" cap like it was a crown.

"Yeah, until we realize we've forgotten snacks, and the only thing we can eat is a gas station hotdog," I shot back, already picturing us sitting in a car with nothing but regret and lukewarm soda.

However, off we went, the dogs in the back seat, practically vibrating with excitement. We had barely left town when Greg took a wrong turn. "I think I took a shortcut," he said sheepishly.

"Shortcut? Or a scenic route through the middle of nowhere?" I replied, noting that our surroundings were becoming increasingly rural. The dogs seemed to think it was an adventure, their heads sticking out of the windows, tongues flapping in the wind.

After getting lost for what felt like a lifetime, we finally ended up at a roadside diner that claimed to have the "World's Best Pie." "You mean the world's best-overpriced slice of disappointment," I laughed as we entered, the smell of fried food assaulting our senses.

Greg ordered a slice of the famous pie, which arrived looking like a slice of a sugar bomb. "Here's to new experiences!" he said, raising his fork as if it were a champagne glass.

As he took a bite, his face contorted into an expression of shock. "I think I just met my pie match," he gasped, reaching for the water glass like it was a lifeline.

"What's it tastes like? Victory?" I asked, snickering.

"More like regret with a side of sugar," he replied, but we both burst into laughter.

Conclusion: Embracing the Absurdity

As the weeks rolled by, Greg and I continued to embrace this new chapter of our lives with open arms and an abundance of laughter. From pottery disasters to cooking capers, our days were filled with spontaneous joy and ridiculous mishaps.

We quickly learned that retirement wasn't just about the absence of work; it was about filling our lives with experiences that made us laugh, even when they turned into total disasters. After all, who needs stability when you can have a lifetime of unpredictable hilarity?

Ice Skating Shenanigans

Eager to kick off our new adventure-filled life, we decided our first escapade would be a trip to the local ice skating rink. Now, let's be honest: neither of us had skated since our younger years, and I had a nagging suspicion that our bodies were far less forgiving than they used to be.

"Just picture it: graceful figures gliding across the ice," Greg said, clutching his skates like they were golden tickets to a magical adventure.

"More like two uncoordinated walruses on a frozen pond," I replied, laughing as we made our way to the rink, our 3 companions Buddy, Honey bear and Murphy trotting behind us, likely judging our life choices.

Once we stepped onto the ice, things went downhill faster than a boulder in a cartoon. Greg wobbled like a newborn giraffe, arms flailing as he tried to find his balance. "I think I'm stuck! Is this how people die?" he shouted, clinging to the wall for dear life.

"Don't panic! Just remember: it's all about the legs. Bend the knees!" I called, but as I turned to demonstrate, I lost my own balance and went down like a sack of potatoes.

"Potatoes, Ruth! You're right! We're definitely in the wrong profession!" Charlie laughed, now attempting to skate in reverse, which looked more like a bizarre dance move than anything remotely graceful.

After several more failed attempts at gliding, we both found ourselves huddled against the wall, gasping for breath between giggles. "Who knew ice skating would turn into an Olympic-level comedy show?" I wheezed.

"I think we'd win the gold medal for most falls per minute!" he replied, wiping tears of laughter from his eyes.

With our dignity in tatters, we decided that perhaps we were better suited for warmer climates. "Next adventure? How about lounging on a beach?" I suggested, imagining the two of us sipping fruity drinks instead of clinging to ice.

Culinary Explorations: The Restaurant Roulette

After our icy escapades, we realized our adventurous spirits were still high. Eager to try something new, we set off on a quest to explore local restaurants we'd never dared to enter. Armed with nothing but our appetites and a questionable sense of direction, we decided to play "restaurant roulette" and flip a coin for our dining destination.

"Flipping for food? Genius!" Greg exclaimed, clearly relishing the thrill of spontaneity.

After a few flips and some silly bets that involved us having to eat something we couldn't pronounce, we landed on a fusion restaurant that promised dishes combining Thai and Italian cuisines. "I'm excited and terrified at the same time!" I said, eyeing the menu with equal parts curiosity and dread.

When the food arrived, we quickly discovered that "fusion" really meant "let's throw everything into a blender and hope for the best." Greg's Pad Thai Pasta looked like an artistic explosion, and I wasn't quite sure whether to eat it or hang it on the wall as modern art.

"Is this what they call 'edible abstract art'?" he chuckled, poking at the noodles with skepticism.

"Looks like a culinary Jackson Pollock masterpiece," I agreed, trying to get a forkful without losing half the plate to the floor.

As we dug in, it became apparent that whoever created this dish had a heavy hand with the spices.

"Oh boy, this is a wild ride!" I gasped, reaching for my water like it was a life raft in a stormy sea.

"Remember, this is a journey of discovery!" Greg said, choking back laughter. "You're supposed to embrace the experience!"

Despite the chaos, we found ourselves laughing more than eating. By the end of our culinary adventure, the floor was littered with napkins, and we had officially broken the record for most 'oops' moments during a meal.

Dog Park Antics: The Canine Chronicles

Emboldened by our restaurant experiences, we decided to take Murphy Buddy and Honey Bear to the local dog park a decision that was both wise and utterly ludicrous. After all, nothing says "fun" like a pack of dogs running wild while their owners try to maintain some semblance of control.

As soon as we arrived, Murphy bounded toward the other dogs like a kid in a candy store, while Buddy ambled along, taking her time to sniff every blade of grass. "Come on, Honey Bear! This is a race, not a leisurely stroll!" Greg called out, but she gave him a look that said, "I'll get there… eventually."

Greg took off after Murphy, who had decided that chasing a squirrel was now his life's mission. I watched, both amused and slightly horrified as Greg flailed after him, arms flapping like a windmill. "I'm not cut out for this!" he shouted, trying to channel his inner dog-whisperer.

In the midst of the chaos, Buddy plopped down beside me, perfectly content to enjoy the sun while the rest of the world went mad. "You get it, don't you, girl?" I said, scratching behind her ears. "Why run when you can lounge?"

Suddenly, an unexpected plot twist occurred: Murphy, fueled by sheer joy and a penchant for trouble, made a beeline for a group of unsuspecting picnickers, stealing a sandwich from the hands of a startled toddler.

"Murphy! NO!" Greg bellowed, breaking into an ungraceful sprint that looked like a scene from a slow-motion movie.

The entire park erupted in laughter as Greg chased after our dog, who was now reveling in his newfound snack. "I swear; we didn't train him to steal!" I called out, barely able to catch my breath from laughing so hard.

Finally, Greg managed to snag Murphy by the collar, bringing him back while the picnic-goers shook their heads in disbelief. "I'm so sorry! He just has an incredible sense of adventure," Greg panted, still trying to regain his composure.

"Oh, we know!" one of the parents laughed. "He's the best entertainment we've had all day!"

SURPRISES ON THE ROAD: A MINI-ROAD TRIP

Feeling invigorated by our dog park exploits, we decided to embark on a spontaneous mini-road trip to the nearby coastal town. "Let's hit the open road! What could possibly go wrong?" I suggested, trying to sound optimistic despite knowing full well our track record.

With a cooler packed with snacks and the dogs comfortably settled in the back, we hit the highway. Greg had meticulously curated a playlist that consisted mostly of 80s classics, and soon we were belting out tunes like we were auditioning for the next big musical.

As we rolled into the town, Greg suddenly veered off the road and into a gas station. "I need snacks! Serious road trip snacks!" he declared, and I couldn't help but giggle at his childlike enthusiasm.

In the store, he emerged with a dubious selection of neon-colored candy and an entire bag of beef jerky. "The essentials!" he proclaimed, holding them aloft like trophies.

After we finally made it to the beach, we were greeted by a sea of beach umbrellas and kids building sandcastles. "This is going to be glorious!" I said, grinning as I kicked off my shoes and ran toward the water.

Just as I reached the waves, a rogue wave crashed over my legs, completely drenching me. "Oh, no! My beautiful shoes!" I shouted, trying to regain my balance but slipping on the wet sand.

Greg doubled over with laughter, attempting to capture the moment on his phone. "You look like a wet seagull!" he teased, holding up the camera for evidence.

"Shut up and help me up!" I replied, half-laughing, half-gasping for air as I flailed in the sand.

Embracing the Joy of New Adventures

As the sun dipped below the horizon, I realized that every new experience was a chance to create lasting memories. With Greg by my side, I felt ready to embrace whatever ridiculous adventure came our way next because in our life together after retirement, every misstep was just another opportunity to laugh, love, and create a unique story worth telling.

"Do you remember when we tried to ice skate and nearly ended up in a hospital?" I asked, resting my head on Greg's shoulder.

"Of course! The hospital might have even given us a trophy for that one," he chuckled.

"I think the real trophy is just making it through each day with you," I said, smiling as the sound of the waves filled the air.

Greg looked at me, eyes sparkling with mischief. "So, what's next on our list of questionable adventures?"

"Maybe skydiving? Or we could try knitting! Who knows?" I grinned, thinking of all the absurd possibilities that lay ahead.

With the world as our oyster, we knew our retirement would be filled with humor, unexpected surprises, and the kind of love that only grows deeper with each shared laugh. So, bring

Chapter 10: The Great Outdoors

Embracing Nature's Quirks

With the novelty of retirement still fresh and our spirits high, Greg and I decided it was time to step outside our comfort zone or, more accurately, step out of our cozy living room and into the great outdoors. Our dogs, Honey Bear, Buddy and Murphy, were ready for the adventure, tails wagging like flags on a battlefield. It felt like we were embarking on an epic quest, armed only with leashes and an overabundance of enthusiasm.

"Let's explore Delaware!" Greg declared one sunny morning, adjusting his sunglasses like a true adventurer. "I hear there are some beautiful parks and beaches nearby."

"Great! Just as long as there aren't any surprise potlucks," I joked, recalling the time we stumbled into a local gathering and left with a Tupperware full of mystery casserole.

"Let's keep our eyes peeled for rogue potato salads," Greg chuckled, and with that, we set off to explore our new surroundings.

THE DOG WALK CHRONICLES

Our first destination was a local park, the kind that boasted rolling hills and a trail that promised to be 'dog-friendly' whatever that meant. As we walked, Greg and I took turns fending off the dogs' enthusiasm. Buddy, our golden retriever, was convinced that every squirrel was her personal mission. Buddy, on the other hand, preferred to take his sweet time sniffing every single blade of grass as if it were a rare artifact.

"Why do you think it takes Honey Bear so long to decide where to go?" Buddy asked, watching Honey Bear engage in a serious debate with a particularly fluffy tuft of grass.

"I think he's contemplating the meaning of life," I replied. "Or perhaps just weighing his options for his next snack."

Buddy eventually decided to launch himself into the nearest bush, emerging triumphant with a stick that was definitely longer than he was. "It's like he thinks he's an ancient warrior bringing home spoils from battle," I laughed.

As we made our way around the park, we encountered other dog walkers. One gentleman, who looked like he had just stepped off a magazine cover, was out with a sleek German shepherd. Greg whispered, "I bet that guy does yoga with his dog."

"Or they share a protein shake after their morning run," I snickered, trying to stifle my laughter as Buddy approached the stylish dog, instantly smitten.

"Do you think our dogs have a dating app?" Greg mused. "Swipe left for the weird ones and right for the sleek ones?"

"I can already picture Buddy's profile," I said, chuckling. "'Likes long naps, philosophy about squirrels, and gourmet grass.'"

As we continued our stroll, I spotted a couple attempting to take a selfie with their poodle, which had other ideas and was determined to chase its tail instead. "I think that poodle is playing hard to get," I remarked, watching them struggle.

"I can relate. Sometimes I feel like I'm chasing my own tail trying to keep up with this retirement thing!" Greg quipped, glancing at Buddy, who had finally decided that the stick was more interesting than the dog park's social scene.

The Beach Trip Disaster

After a few weeks of park adventures, we decided to hit the beach. Greg had insisted that a day by the water would be refreshing. "Plus, the dogs love the beach!" he assured me, pulling out a cooler filled with snacks.

"I love how you have snacks for both us and the dogs," I replied, rolling my eyes. "I just hope the dogs don't think it's a buffet."

Once we arrived at the beach, the scenery was stunning golden sand, sparkling waves, and an abundance of seagulls. As we set up our spot, Honey Bear was off like a shot, dashing towards the water as if it were the final frontier. Buddy, however, remained skeptical. He inched forward cautiously, like a seasoned detective on a crime scene.

"Come on, Buddy! It's just water!" Greg called, beckoning him to join Honey Bear.

"I think he's worried he'll find out what happens to the stick when it gets wet," I joked.

The moment Honey Bear hit the water, she transformed into a majestic, albeit muddy, dolphin. She leapt through the waves, her golden fur glistening in the sun, while Buddy stood firmly on dry land, peering into the water like it was a portal to another dimension.

"I think he's judging Honey Bear's life choices," I said, chuckling as Buddy tilted his head, evaluating her sea-splashed enthusiasm.

Greg and I took turns playing with Honey Bear, who was clearly living her best life. But just as I was getting into the spirit, I caught sight of the incoming tide. "Greg! The water!" I shouted, trying to warn him before the waves caught us both off guard.

We scrambled, barely escaping the sudden splash, and I ended up half-soaked, laughing uncontrollably. "I didn't sign up for a swim lesson!" I gasped between giggles.

"Welcome to the 'Greg and Ruth Water Sports Academy,'" Greg laughed, wringing out his shirt. "Next up: synchronized splashing!"

The tide continued to roll in, and I soon realized that beach trips with two exuberant dogs were like playing a high-stakes game of dodgeball. Just when you thought you were safe, a wave would sneak up and drench you, or one of the dogs would run by and send sand flying everywhere.

"Is this the fun you promised?" I yelled, trying to keep my balance as Honey Bear launched herself at a flock of seagulls.

"I swear I'm not trying to drown you!" Greg shouted back, laughing so hard he nearly fell over.

WILDLIFE ENCOUNTERS

On one of our subsequent dog walks, we became fascinated by the local wildlife. Greg, in his newfound retirement wisdom, decided we should try birdwatching. "It'll be fun!" he insisted, brandishing a pair of binoculars he'd bought on sale.

"Right. Fun. As long as the birds don't judge my lack of bird knowledge," I replied, rolling my eyes but secretly intrigued.

We set out, armed with a bird guide and an impressive amount of snacks. "If we see a cardinal, we can toast to its red beauty!" Greg proclaimed, flipping through the guide as we walked.

An hour later, we were sitting on a park bench, binoculars at the ready, and I was beginning to wonder if we were better suited for the couch than the wilderness. "Look!" Greg suddenly exclaimed, pointing at a bird that was more interested in a pile of leaves than our excitement.

"Is that even a real bird?" I asked, squinting through the binoculars. "It looks like it just rolled out of bed and forgot to comb its feathers."

"Ah, yes! The elusive 'Disheveled Duck,' a rare species indeed!" Greg joked, causing me to burst into laughter.

As we continued our adventure, I spotted a squirrel attempting to steal food from a picnic basket nearby. "Look at that little thief!" I said, pointing.

"Maybe we should take him home as a new pet," Greg replied. "He could be our 'delightful little bandit.'"

"You mean our next retired roommate?" I shot back. "He'd probably charge rent in acorns!"

Our laughter echoed through the park as we witnessed nature's antics unfold before us. We even began to make up stories about the animals we saw, creating elaborate backstories for every creature.

"See that bird over there? He's a retired pilot," I said, watching a pigeon strut by. "He's decided to hang up his wings and enjoy the slower life of loafing around parks."

"Of course! And that squirrel? He's a former hedge fund manager who lost it all in a nut market crash," Greg added, gesturing dramatically.

"Together, they run a support group for wayward wildlife!" I chimed in, and we both erupted into giggles, blissfully lost in our imaginations.

EMBRACING THE CHARM OF DELAWARE

Through all our adventures, we began to appreciate the unique charm of Delaware. "It's quirky and unpredictable," I mused one evening while watching the sunset from our patio, the dogs sprawled out beside us.

"It's like us! Quirky and unpredictable," Greg replied, raising an imaginary glass. "To Delaware!"

"To Delaware! And to retirement! Who knew we'd be having this much fun?" I raised my cup of tea, clinking it against his glass of lemonade.

We took a moment to soak it all in our life was a tapestry of absurdities, laughter, and the unwavering bond we shared. It was a celebration of embracing the unknown, of exploring new experiences together, and relishing the little joys life had to offer.

Unforgettable Quirks

One day, we decided to visit a local farm to pick fresh strawberries, thinking it would be a romantic outing. Armed with sun hats and excitement, we headed out, picturing ourselves as the star couple in a farm-themed rom-com.

As we approached the berry patch, I had visions of picturesque baskets brimming with ripe, juicy strawberries. Instead, we discovered a field of eager children darting around, plucking berries faster than we could keep up.

"Looks like we've entered the 'Hunger Games' of strawberry picking," I muttered, watching a toddler dash by with a bucket half-filled with berries, while another was in a standoff with a chicken.

Charlie snorted. "If they give us any trouble, just tell them we're seasoned berry hunters."

After several hilarious moments of dodging kids and chickens, we finally found our stride. I started tossing strawberries into the basket, feeling like a champion. "Look at us! We're practically farmers!"

But then disaster struck. In my enthusiasm, I didn't notice Buddy had found his way to the berry patch. Suddenly, there was chaos. Greg's voice turned from jovial to alarmed as Buddy, convinced he had found the ultimate treasure, decided to make a beeline for the strawberries.

"Buddy, no!" Greg shouted, chasing after him. I couldn't help but laugh as Buddy joyfully bounded through the patch, leaving a trail of crushed strawberries in his wake.

"Should we just call this a 'fruit salad fiasco'?" I laughed, trying to keep my balance while navigating the berry explosion.

"Or 'The Great Strawberry Catastrophe!'" Charlie replied, laughing as he finally caught up to Buddy, who was now contentedly sitting amidst the wreckage, tongue lolling out in satisfaction.

We ended the day with sunburns and a whole lot of laughter, clutching our hard-earned strawberry haul a testament to our ongoing adventures.

THE ADVENTURE CONTINUES

As summer unfolded, Greg and I continued to explore Delaware, sharing laughter and love with every step we took. Each adventure, no matter how trivial, became a story etched in our hearts a reminder that life after retirement could be filled with unexpected joy, connection, and more than a few funny mishaps.

"Who knew that the great outdoors would become our playground?" Greg said one night, as we reminisced about our escapades.

"And who knew that a dog named Buddy would become our unofficial adventure guide?" I replied, leaning against him, grateful for the journey we were on together.

With a twinkle in his eye, Greg nodded. "Here's to more adventures, more laughter, and yes, maybe even more berry disasters."

"Absolutely! Just as long as we don't get stuck in a potato salad situation again!"

And with that, we clinked our glasses, ready to embrace whatever adventures awaited us in the great, quirky outdoors of Delaware.

Chapter 11: Life Lessons and Reflections

The Journey So Far

As Greg and I settled into our cozy living room one evening, I couldn't help but gaze out the window at the sunset painting the sky in vibrant hues of orange and pink. This tranquil moment was a stark contrast to the whirlwind of laughter, mischief, and delightful absurdities we'd embraced since retiring. I took a sip of my herbal tea and turned to Greg, who was rummaging through his "retirement treasure chest" a.k.a. a drawer filled with assorted dog toys and an alarming number of novelty socks.

"Can you believe it? We're actually living the dream!" I exclaimed, recalling the countless escapades we'd experienced, from chaotic beach trips to the dog park that felt more like a comedy club.

Greg looked up, wearing a mismatched pair of socks one with donuts and the other with dancing cats. "Living the dream or living the meme? Either way, it's quite the adventure," he replied, chuckling.

"Absolutely! And it's filled with lessons. Speaking of which, do you remember that time we thought we could master paddle boarding?" I asked, stifling a laugh as I recalled the hilarity of that day.

COMEDIC REFLECTIONS ON AGING

"Ah, yes! The great paddle boarding debacle," Greg grinned, leaning back in his chair. "That was quite the spectacle. I don't think I've ever seen someone try to balance on a board while being pelted by the waves and our dogs!"

"Hey, in our defense, we thought it would be a relaxing outing. We didn't anticipate the 'splash zone' to be an Olympic event," I said, laughing as I remembered Honey Bear's enthusiastic attempts to help.

With a gleam in his eye, Greg continued, "And there you were, trying to maintain your balance while Buddy decided that the board was actually a trampoline. You practically performed a somersault off that thing!"

"Right? I was only a few seconds away from becoming a viral sensation!" I added, shaking my head at the memory. "But honestly, isn't that what growing older is all about? Embracing the absurd and laughing at ourselves?"

Greg nodded, "Absolutely! Who knew that aging could feel like a sitcom? I mean, every week feels like an episode of 'Greg and Ruth: The Retired Chronicles.'"

"Complete with unexpected guest stars like our neighbor's cat," I quipped, remembering the time Mr. Whiskers had decided to join our dog walks, much to Buddy's horror.

"Ah, yes! The 'Cat Who Thought He Was a Dog' episode. That was classic!" Greg laughed. "Who knew our dog would take so much offense to sharing the spotlight?"

HEARTWARMING ANECDOTES OF FRIENDSHIP AND LOVE

Amid our laughter, the warmth of our memories enveloped us like a well-worn blanket. I reflected on the friendships we had forged since moving to Delaware. Each friend had brought a unique flavor to our lives, like a delightful potluck of personalities.

"There's something magical about this community, don't you think?" I mused, recalling the many dinners, game nights, and spontaneous gatherings we'd enjoyed.

Greg nodded. "Absolutely. The way everyone rallies around each other is heartwarming. Like that time, we organized a 'Help Your Neighbor' day and ended up with a barbecue instead of a clean-up!"

"Or when we tried to start a book club but ended up spending more time talking about our favorite ice cream flavors than the actual book!" I added, grinning at the memory.

"Exactly! And it's those moments of connection that remind me how blessed we are," Greg said, his expression turning reflective. "We've built a life filled with laughter, love, and some seriously questionable choices."

"Speaking of questionable choices, remember when we thought we could start gardening?" I said, shaking my head at the memory of our poor, wilted plants. And oh, by the way I named my plant (Ficus is named Sherman and my Zzplant is call Morterimer

"Ha! I think our plants might have been the real victims in that experiment," Greg chuckled. "I'm pretty sure they were trying to escape!"

With a warm smile, I added, "But even with our gardening fiasco, we learned that growing together is what matters. Even if our plants were more of a 'lost cause' than a 'growing success.'"

AGING: FUNNY AND LIBERATING

As we reflected on our adventures, a sense of liberation washed over me. Aging wasn't just about wrinkles and gray hairs; it was about embracing the freedom to be ourselves, ridiculousness included.

"I think we've finally realized that we can do whatever we want!" I proclaimed. "We can be goofy, spontaneous, and let our dogs lead us on adventures. Who needs a grand plan when we have this beautiful chaos?"

Greg raised his cup, his expression gleeful. "To chaos and the beauty of growing older! Who knew getting older could be so liberating?"

"Right? And can we talk about how liberating it is to wear mismatched socks in public without a care?" I grinned, gesturing to Greg's outrageous footwear.

"Exactly! It's the little things that make life joyous," Greg said, tapping my cup with his. "Let's embrace our quirks, our moments of hilarity, and the heartwarming connections we've made along the way."

The Blessing of a Happy Life

As we reminisced about our journey, the thought of how blessed we were struck me. We had built a life overflowing with love, laughter, and a genuine appreciation for the absurdities we encountered.

"Do you ever think about how lucky we are?" I asked, my voice softening. "To have each other, our dogs, and this community? It's a blessing."

Greg nodded, his eyes warm. "Every single day. I never thought retirement would feel this fulfilling. It's like we're writing our own story, and I wouldn't want anyone else by my side."

With a smile, I added, "And it's a story that's filled with humor, heart, and a lot of chaos. Just like life itself!"

As I gazed at Greg, I felt an overwhelming wave of affection wash over me. Here was my partner in crime, my confidant, and the one person who made every day feel like a new adventure. It wasn't just about the grand gestures; it was about the small moments, like sharing a laugh over burnt toast or fighting for the last piece of chocolate.

The Legacy of Laughter

As the sun dipped below the horizon, casting a golden glow through our window, I felt an overwhelming sense of gratitude. We had navigated this adventure called life together, learning, growing, and laughing through every twist and turn.

In that moment, I realized that it wasn't just the big moments that defined us but the laughter we shared during the ordinary ones. Whether we were paddle boarding disasters or experiencing "the great strawberry caper," it was those tiny fragments of joy that made our lives extraordinary.

"Let's make a pact," I suggested, my heart full. "No matter where this journey takes us, let's promise to keep laughing, keep exploring, and keep finding the absurdity in every moment."

"Deal!" Greg replied, grinning ear to ear. "To the adventures ahead!"

With our glasses raised once more, we celebrated the lessons we had learned, the friendships we cherished, and the beautiful, chaotic life we had built together. It was a life filled with love, laughter, and a commitment to embracing the journey, no matter how absurd it may be. And as we clinked our cups, I knew that this was just the beginning of the next chapter one filled with humor, heart, and a touch of madness.

THE GOLDEN YEARS: MORE THAN JUST A PHASE

"Let's face it," I said, settling into the couch with a content sigh. "The golden years aren't just about retirement; they're about finding joy in every silly little moment, whether it's watching our dogs chase their tails or debating the best flavor of ice cream."

"Absolutely! Who knew that in our golden years, we'd become the local experts on dog antics and ice cream flavors? "Greg laughed, his eyes sparkling. "I mean; did you ever think we'd be competing with the neighborhood kids over the last scoop of mint chocolate chip?"

I chuckled. "And losing, might I add! I think they have an unfair advantage with their youthful energy."

"True, but we have experience on our side!" Greg declared. "We've spent decades honing our skills in the fine art of 'strategic snack acquisition.'"

"Let's not forget our secret weapon our dogs!" I said. "They're the perfect distraction! While the kids are busy petting them, we swoop in and grab the last scoop of ice cream."

Greg feigned a dramatic gasp. "Ruth, are you suggesting we use our dogs as decoys for dessert? This is genius!"

"Desperate times call for desperate measures!" I exclaimed, laughter bubbling up. "But in all seriousness, it's moments like these that remind me how rich our lives are now. We might not have a schedule or a boss to impress, but we have each other and all the joy we can muster."

THE CIRCLE OF FRIENDSHIP

As the evening wore on, I found myself thinking about the friendships we had cultivated since our retirement. Each one felt like a new layer added to our lives, a rich tapestry woven from shared laughter and support.

"Do you remember that time we hosted that neighborhood potluck?" I asked, bursting with the memory. "I thought it was going to be a disaster, but it turned into a comedy show."

Greg snorted. "You mean when you accidentally set the casserole on fire while trying to impress everyone with your 'secret family recipe'?"

I groaned dramatically. "I still can't believe that happened! And you, with your nonchalant 'don't worry, we can always order pizza,' made it even worse. I was mortified!"

"Hey, you handled it like a champ! And the way everyone rallied around you? That was heartwarming," Charlie replied. "Not to mention the look on your face when you realized our friends were more interested in the fire extinguisher than the food!"

"True! They definitely turned that disaster into a memorable moment," I said, my heart swelling with affection for our friends. "And it's those experiences that have created bonds that feel unbreakable. We've created a community here, and I cherish that."

Cherishing Every Moment

As we settled into the evening, I took a moment to appreciate the serenity of our home, the laughter echoing in the walls, and the love that enveloped us. The lessons learned through laughter and absurdity had shaped our lives in ways we never expected.

"Here's to more adventures!" I declared, raising my cup in a toast. "More laughter, more friends, and, yes, more culinary disasters!"

"Cheers to that!" Greg grinned clinking his cup against mine.

In that moment, I felt a profound sense of peace wash over me. Retirement wasn't just an end; it was a beautiful beginning, a chance to savor life in all its imperfect glory. Together, Greg and I were crafting a life filled with stories, each one a testament to the power of love, laughter, and the joy of embracing the unexpected.

As the stars twinkled in the night sky, I knew that whatever lay ahead, we would face it together with humor, heart, and a generous sprinkle of absurdity. And I couldn't think of anyone else I'd rather share this extraordinary journey with than Greg.

www.ingramcontent.com/pod-product-compliance
Lightning Source LLC
Chambersburg PA
CBHW072114050526
44107CB00098BA/174